POLICE
IN AMERICA

THE POLICEWOMAN

Her Service and Ideals

Mary E. Hamilton

ARNO PRESS & THE NEW YORK TIMES
NEW YORK, 1971

Reprint Edition 1971 by Arno Press Inc.

LC# 74-154596
ISBN 0-405-03370-2

Police In America
ISBN for complete set: 0-405-03360-5
See last pages of this volume for titles.

Manufactured in the United States of America

THE POLICEWOMAN

HER SERVICE AND IDEALS

THE POLICEWOMAN
HER SERVICE AND IDEALS

BY

MARY E. HAMILTON

"To cure is the voice of the past,
To prevent, the divine whisper of today."

NEW YORK
FREDERICK A. STOKES COMPANY
MCMXXIV

I DEDICATE THIS BOOK
TO
POLICEWOMEN
WHOSE SERVICE AND IDEALS ARE
CONSECRATED TO THE GREAT
CAUSE OF HUMANITY

AUTHOR'S NOTE

The following is not a historical survey; it is merely an account of police work as I, a woman, have experienced it, together with my observations and views on the subject generally. The purpose in presenting such a book is twofold. It is hoped that it may serve in a way as a guide to women who enter the field and also give all people a better understanding of what women can do along these lines and how greatly they are needed in working out the problems which have to do with the betterment of human conditions through police protection and crime prevention.

PREFACE

Experience is the great teacher of us all, but for the American policewoman there has practically been no other guide. Policewomanship is still such a new profession for women that those who have undertaken it have had to depend largely upon what they have learned from doing other things, common sense and that intangible heritage of woman—Instinct.

Even today when the idea of having policewomen is an accepted, established one, people still ask: "What must one do to become a policewoman? Why do we have policewomen?" These questions are significant of a lack of standardization in the organization of policewomen's work, which until accomplished will retard its progress. It is not unusual to find the policewomen of one city following a policy diametrically opposed to that of another city. It is incumbent upon the pioneers among us to recount our experiences so that all may understand the great responsibility and opportunity for service offered to the policewoman of today and follow along the same way.

If all the pioneer policewomen were to submit a summary of their experience prior to their taking up police work, we would have a most interesting human document, one from which might be gleaned all the necessary qualifications that a woman, who wishes to be a good policewoman, should possess.

Looking back upon my own experience I feel that my preparation for the work began thirty years ago when I accepted my first position. It had to do with the investigation of tenement house conditions and I, acting in the capacity of secretary for a group of notable men, organized in Boston as the Anti-Tenement House League, was brought in contact for the first time with social service. If I were asked to choose a foundation upon which to build a strong force of policewomen, Social Service would be the corner stone.

It must have been an inward urge to work with people that carried me into industry, for I found myself entering this field early in my career only to leave it when, after twenty years of service, I was eligible for retirement. The industrial world in which I worked for so many years was an excellent training school for my later public service. Being an artist as well as a skilled artisan, my workshop had to be a beautiful, harmonious world and to make it so I was continually obliged to adjust conditions and combat sinister forces. The labor upon which I depended for my output was for the most part that of young girls and women whom poor or unhappy circumstances had thrown into the market without preparation or training. Hence along with the task of securing a fair day's work for a fair day's pay, I was confronted by every possible social problem. It was here that I learned a lesson which has served me in all my dealings with people both good and bad, and that is, to help people one must first win their confidence and friendship. It is particularly important for a policewoman to adopt this attitude, for more good can be accomplished by women in police work along lines of prevention and protection than by force.

Courses at the School of Philanthropy and New York University did much to round out my practical experience, but that which had the greatest educative value and has aided me most in my present work, is the rearing of a son from babyhood to manhood. To do effective police work, a woman must understand the child's point of view and appreciate the difficulties of adolescence, and who but a mother has a better opportunity of acquiring this sympathy and understanding?

With the World War arose many unusual situations and among them were serious problems having to do with the protection and wel-

fare of children, girls and women. It was
at this crucial time that all women came for-
ward to offer their aid in whatever field they
were most needed. I am glad that I was assigned to the novel and difficult task of being
New York City's first policewoman. Today
there are one hundred women officers in the
Police Department of New York City, thirty
of whom are patrolwomen. We are all
pioneers in a new and wonderful service, the
aim of which is the improvement of human
conditions through crime prevention and protection. There is much to be done and all
that we have yet done is just a beginning.

CONTENTS

[xv]

FOREWORD

Ten years ago, in connection with the field
work for my book "American Police Systems," I had the opportunity of visiting over
a hundred police departments in the United
States from Boston to Los Angeles. At that
time the policewoman represented an innovation in police work and in only a few cities had
the idea been introduced. Even in those few
cities there was no conception of the place in
the department which the policewoman would
occupy. She was added to the force only because the Chiefs of Police wanted to be able
to say that their departments were up to date.
I remember in one city the Chief of Police,
in great bewilderment, was trying to teach his
six new policewomen to shoot pistols—without great success—and to learn the intricacies

of handling an eighteen-inch club. He confessed to me that when these accomplishments were finally acquired he intended to place the women on beats in precincts "where conditions were not too rough."

Mrs. Hamilton's interesting book shows the tremendous development in the use of policewomen. Beginning in the crude way which I have indicated, the whole emphasis has been shifted, and the policewoman has become one of the chief agents of the community not only in the prevention of crime but in the protection of those who are too often the victims of crime.

Mrs. Hamilton's vivid little book gives a most interesting picture of this development and suggests the principles for its sound expansion.

RAYMOND B. FOSDICK.

233 Broadway
New York City
February 8, 1924.

THE POLICEWOMAN
HER SERVICE AND IDEALS

The Policewoman

HER SERVICE AND IDEALS

CHAPTER I

WOMAN'S PLACE IN THE DEPARTMENT

THERE was a time, not many years ago, when a Police Department was No Woman's Land. As in other professions, police work was distinctly a man's job; the proper sphere for woman was the home.

Today the idea of employing policewomen is an accepted one and their presence on the force does not seem more unusual than any other modern innovation.

This new profession for women is without doubt only a part of a great movement which has awakened womankind to a fuller realization of their responsibility towards society and the need of their taking an active part in the affairs of the community. In assuming these larger interests women have not forsaken the home ideals, but invariably work out their programs and develop their activities in accordance with the traditions of the home and to this may be attributed much of the success of women in their work today.

In many ways the position of a women in a police department is not unlike that of a mother in a home. Just as a mother smoothes out the rough places, looks after the children and gives a timely word of warning, advice or encouragement, so the policewoman fulfills her duty.

Police officers are largely concerned with law enforcement, preservation of the public peace and the protection of life and property. For a long time policemen have performed these duties nobly and even today without the faithful surveillance of our brave bluecoats,

[4]

civilization might be in a turmoil. Why, then, are policewomen necessary? The best answer to this question is Progress.

When public spirited groups and individuals began to realize that the best way to solve some of the most difficult police problems was by preventing crime and that such prevention logically started with children, a big advance in police work was made. It was then that the need for policewomen arose. With *Prevention and Protection* as a slogan and the welfare of children, girls and women for their field of service, policewomen have been given a task to perform quite different from that of their fellow policemen. Raymond Fosdick once said that when policewomen put on uniforms, carried guns and clubs they became little men, but when they did their work as women, they rendered a great service. And it is certainly a fact that no woman can really be a good policewoman, unless she works as a woman and carries with her into a police department a woman's ideals.

[5]

A woman's way of dealing with a problem is oftentimes wholly unlike a man's method of working out the same thing. Both may be good, but there are without doubt some police problems, particularly those in which the affairs of children, girls and women are involved, that can best be handled by a policewoman merely because of the fact that she is a woman. For instance in the cases of women and girls, all interviews relating to sex are matters demanding the attention of policewomen. Just as a mother discusses these things with her daughters instead of delegating the duty to the father, so a policewoman, when it is necessary to do so, should discuss such topics rather than the policeman.

The rules and regulations, customs and traditions of police departments, having developed completely under the regime of men do not always function according to a woman's way of doing things. To attempt to accomplish everything one would like to do by disregarding the system in operation, would be

[6]

a very unwise policy for policewomen to adopt. Effective service depends largely upon the extent to which the women co-operate with the men, for after all, police-women have taken up policewomanship, not with the idea of replacing men in this work, but for the purpose of aiding and assisting them by seeking in a quiet, unassuming way to prevent crime. As soon as a policewoman proves by her good works that she is sincere, honest and earnest, any antagonism that the men may be inclined to display at first quickly vanishes.

Within recent years New York and another large eastern city have employed police-women for the first time. The policy of New York illustrates the right way of using the service of women in police work; that of the other city as the newspapers reported it, shows the wrong way.

In New York City, the first policewoman was a volunteer worker who had been trained at a school of Social Science. The services

[7]

of an officially appointed woman had been requested by various prominent organizations on the grounds that a woman protective officer could best look after the welfare of the girls of the city. It was then that the famous Bureau of Missing Persons was in an embryo stage and in developing this work it was essential that a woman be assigned to many of the missing girls cases. Generally the men in the service, did not favor the idea of women entering the field. Not until some difficult cases had been closed satisfactorily by the new appointee did they change their opinion and accept the woman as a regular full fledged policewoman.

When the first policewoman was appointed to a position in the New York Police Department the fact was not concealed. The men knew who she was, understood why she was there and looked upon her as a fellow worker, who was simply tackling the problem from a different angle. The result has been that policewomen in New York have been a success and have proven a help to the Department in every way. New York will always have policewomen.

A short time ago a policewoman in the other city resigned her position because she objected to the duties that had been assigned her, which were in the nature of gathering evidence. "I had joined the force," she said, "to help fallen women and wayward children. Instead I was forced to accompany men of the lowest type, professional stool pigeons, around town, to enter dives of the worst type and do work which could be done much better by men."

The idea of this city was to make of their women, not protective officers, but detectives. When the women were first appointed, they patrolled the various posts of the patrolmen unbeknown to these officers. Such a procedure in itself was sufficient to arouse the suspicion of the men and prejudice them against the women for all time. One newspaper reporter tersely analyzed the situation

[9]

as follows: "The work of the new police-women so far appears to be of the watchful waiting order with considerable difficulty in killing time. It looks as though waiting for some one to be bad was going to be a deadly monotonous job for our women's police force." With such a beginning it is not surprising that the outcome of the experiment should register such complete failure as was indicated by the resignation of a woman who had the right ideas about the kind of police work a woman should do, but was given no opportunity to develop her good ideas.

Besides the successes and failures we have the cities who see the light and want police-women and those who are still in darkness and refuse to appoint women as police officers. Paterson, New Jersey, for instance endorsed the policewomen movement heartily because the people there realized that only by the ap-pointment of policewomen could the prob-lems presented by the large numbers of girl operatives in the Paterson silk mills and the children of foreign families be handled properly. A womens' league of a large Connecticut city, on the other hand, by resolutions violently denounced the attempts that were being made to appoint policewomen in that city, because they did not believe a woman could do police duty "with the ability, efficiency and promptness of a man." It would be interesting to compare conditions in Paterson with those of this city without policewomen or perhaps to enlighten the ladies who oppose the measure by statistics showing the number of wayward or runaway girls from that city, who are ably, efficiently and promptly handled by policewomen when they leave home and come to New York for a little jaunt.

If the value of policewomen is to be measured in dollars and cents, there may be cities who will follow London's blind lead and declare that women police are too costly to maintain. But when the work of policewomen is appraised in terms of Lives—the lives of children, young girls and women—more and more cities and towns will want policewomen at any cost.

"Police work is no longer a matter of hand-cuffs and truncheons," said Lady Astor, in pleading for the continuance of women police in London, "but of prevention of crime as much as possible, and the preventive work that has been already done by the women police, even with their limited powers, is a piece of national economy which it would be hard to beat.

"Surely it is better and cheaper to give stranded girls warning and advice, and to find them shelter, than to allow them to drift until they become charges on the community as short-sentence prisoners and gradually degenerate into habitual criminals.

"The value of the women police will never be fully realized until the whole question of dealing with women of the unfortunate class is put into the hands of women. When that is done the community will reap the full benefit of their services."

STANDARDS

CHAPTER II

STANDARDS

IN 1921, a large eastern city published in its official bulletin a list of fifty-five male applicants for the position of patrolman. The following were their previous occupations: Clerk, electrician, special officer, driver, chauffeur, junk dealer, boiler maker, guard, salesman, machinist, longshoreman, sand paperer, conductor, deck hand, printer, tile layer's helper, foreman, painter, feeder, oiler, helper, soldier, signalman, porter, caster, holder-on, iron moulder, installer and bartender. It does not necessarily follow that these men would not make good policemen because their former occupations, for the most part, had not prepared them especially for the work, but it does show that the standards fixed for policewomen must be higher, since a woman, if she possesses the qualifications now demanded for the position of police officer, would necessarily have to have had experience more along the line of police work and clearly these vocations for the most part do not indicate such experience.

Although there is still considerable divergence of opinion as to just what the requisites for the office of policewoman should be, it is generally agreed that women seeking to do this work should be fitted by age, education, experience, temperament, physical strength and physique to fulfill the strenuous duties required of them.

An age limit is necessarily set for new applicants, usually the minimum age being around twenty-one with a maximum of thirty-five or forty. In a well balanced force of policewomen, there is a place for workers of all ages providing they possess all other qualifications. Oftentimes the services of a young woman are needed; again a case demands a

woman of mature years. Really the adage—
a woman is as old as she looks—might well
apply to policewomen, for actual age matters
little; it is more important that a woman possess mature judgment and still retain a youthful point of view.

While intelligence is an essential attribute
and a trained mind one of the biggest assets
that a modern policewoman can have, these
need not be acquired by all in the same way.
High school training is a good beginning, a
college education is certainly one of the most
direct ways of attaining these qualifications
and yet to set such a compulsory educational
standard would exclude some of the ablest
women that have joined the forces. It is possible for some people to acquire an education
without the formal attendance at school and
any woman whose teacher has been Experience is invariably an invaluable aid in this
work, for she knows how to surmount difficulties and is schooled to depend upon her
own resources.

It is interesting to see how varied are the ideas of the numerous towns and cities employing policewomen, when it comes to their determining what training a woman should have to qualify her for police work. In some places it is frankly admitted that no previous training is required; others go to the extreme of insisting upon college training, while many take a sensible middle course and say that an applicant should at least have a high school education.

Social service training and physical fitness are generally emphasized. Where the position of policewomen has been standardized to the extent of having been made a civil service position, the requirements have been worked out most carefully and conform to the usual standards set for patrolmen.

On May 13, 1921, the first civil service examination for Patrolwomen in the Police Department of New York City was given under the rules and regulations of the Municipal Civil Service Commission. The following notice of the examination shows a carefully planned set of requirements:

MUNICIPAL CIVIL SERVICE COMMISSION
Notice of Examination

PUBLIC NOTICE IS HEREBY GIVEN THAT applications will be received by the Municipal Civil Service Commission, Municipal Building, Manhattan, New York City, from

Tuesday, March 1, 1921, to Tuesday, March 15. 1921,

for the position of

Patrolwoman, Police Department,

A New Position Created by Chapter 509 of the Laws of 1920.

All examinations are open to both men and women unless otherwise stated.

No applications delivered at the office of the Commission, by mail or otherwise, after 4 p. m., Tuesday, March 15, 1921, will be accepted. Application blanks will be mailed upon request provided a self-addressed stamped envelope or sufficient postage is inclosed to cover the mailing. The Commission will not guarantee the delivery of the same. Postage on applications forwarded by mail must be fully prepaid.

Notice of the dates of the various parts of this examination will be published in the "City Record."

The term of eligibility of the list resulting from this examination is fixed at not less than one year nor more than four years.

The Policewoman

Applicants must be citizens of the United States and residents of the State of New York.

Persons appointed from the eligible list resulting from this examination become members of the retirement system described in Chapter XXVI of the Charter, voluntarily within six months, and compulsorily after six months of service.

Applications for this examination must be filed on Form D.

The subjects and weights of the examination are: Experience, 2, Oral, 3; 70 per cent required. Duties, 4; 70 per cent required. Citizenship, 1. 70 per cent general average required.

The subject Citizenship is designed to test the relative merit and fitness of candidates for appointment by reason of good citizenship as shown by military, marine or naval service under the Federal or State governments, length of domicile in the City of New York, and general character and reputation. The rating on this subject will be ascertained from the candidate's sworn statement which is to be filed on a special blank. Full particulars as to rating will be described on such blank.

A qualifying physical examination will be given.

Duties: The moral protection of women and minors; the prevention of delinquency among women and minors; and the performance of such other duties as the Police Commissioner may assign.

Requirements: Experience in probation work, and in the care, reformation or relief of women and minors, will receive special consideration; graduation from a recognized school for trained nurses, or a normal school will also be considered a desirable qualification.

Standards

The oral examination will be thorough. It is desired to secure candidates possessing the dignity and force of character to exercise a strong beneficient influence on women and minors and who also possess the ability to prevent and detect crime.

No woman shall be eligible for appointment as Patrolwoman who is less than 21 years or more than 35 years of age on date of filing her application for Civil Service examination.

Applicants will be required to submit with the applications a transcript of the records of the Bureau of Vital Statistics, showing the date of birth, or in lieu thereof, an authenticated transcript from the records of the church in which they were baptized, or other satisfactory proof.

All foreign-born applicants will be required to submit evidence of citizenship. Naturalization papers should be attached to the application. Applicants must be not less than 5 feet 2 inches in height and at this height must weigh 120 pounds.

Entrance salary, $1,769 per annum.*
Vacancies occur from time to time.

CHARLES I. STENGLE, Secretary.

The questions of this examination also give a very clear idea of the kind of experience that is expected of applicants and the scope of

---

*In November, 1923, a measure for the increase of patrolmen's salary to a minimum of $2,500 was passed by popular vote. Under the Civil Service Laws Patrolwomen have the same right and privileges of patrolmen.

a policewoman's duties in any large city. The following is the particular examination paper in question:

MUNICIPAL CIVIL SERVICE COMMISSION
New York.

These questions are to be taken only for what they are. Questions actually set for the position named. For future examinations question will be framed to suit the requirements of the position at the time of the examination.

PATROLWOMAN—POLICE DEPARTMENT
Date: May 13, 1921.

Duties—Weight 4

Part I
To be finished by 12:30 P. M.

1.　　Discuss the so-called "commercial" dance hall as a factor in the downfall of girls and state fully the police attention these places should receive.

2.   (a) Define "juvenile deliquency" accord-
        ing to the law.

    (b) Of what use are the so-called Big
        Brothers and Big Sisters in your
        opinion?

    (c) What is meant by "the age of con-
        sent?" What is the "age of con-
        sent in this state?"

    (d) Describe the manner in which child-
        ren are linked up with the traffic
        in habit-forming drugs in New
        York City.

3.   (a) State specifically the advice you, as
        a Patrolwoman, would offer in a
        case where one member of a poor
        family is suspected of having con-
        tracted the most serious of venereal
        diseases.

    (b) In your opinion what various spe-
        cific acts or conditions could prop-
        erly be prosecuted under the gen-
        eral charge of "impairing the
        morals of a minor?"

4.　　　To what city departments or bureaus or other agencies should the following be referred?

(a) Complaint alleging fraud on the part of a public employment agency.

(b) Request for legal advice regarding the best means of protecting a poor family from an avaricious landlord.

(c) Complaint about the inadequate heating of an apartment house during the winter months.

(d) Requests for aid in obtaining employment.

(e) Complaint alleging the giving of short weight by a retail dealer.

(f) Request for the commitment of children to some institution in a case where the parents are unable, though willing, to support them.

(g) Request for advice as to what should be done with the personal property of a man who died without leaving a will.

5. (a) In your opinion what constitutes "mashing" as an offense or practice of which the police of this city should take cognizance?

(b) Where are "mashers" likely to be met with and what are the usual methods they employ?

Part II

To be finished at 3:30 P. M.

6. (a) Name and locate the passenger railroad terminals situated within the limits of New York City. State the more important cities or towns to which the railroad lines run from each of these terminals.

(b) Name the various steamboat or excursion boat lines that operate between New York City and nearby places throughout the year or during certain seasons of the year. Locate the terminus (landing place) of each line in New York City and state the places to which these boats run.

(c) Name and locate the large public parks in New York City.

(d) Name and locate the favorite outdoor commercial amusement places in New York City.

7. State the nature of the relief, if any, that can be afforded the persons named below and give, step by step, the procedure to be followed in order that the relief may be obtained.

(a) An unmarried mother.

(b) A dependent widow, who is a citizen of the United States and who has lived in New York City for the past five years. (Note: The husband of this woman died recently.)

(c) A blind adult, supported by his

brother and sister who are poor working people.

8. What types or classes of criminals or offenders against the law use minors as aides in the commission of crimes or the carrying on of nefarious practices and what classes or types of persons are accustomed to annoy children or prey upon them? Discuss fully.

9. (a) For what particular conditions or circumstances should a keen, observant Patrolwoman be on the outlook in the following places?

1. A congested summer bungalow colony inhabited by the working class and containing many bungalows run by young men's social clubs.

2. A plain neighborhood, containing cheap furnished room houses almost exclusively, and bordering on a busy thoroughfare where there are grouped several of the

lower-class theatres, a passenger railroad terminal and two or three business schools.

3. A cheap motion picture theatre in a neighborhood inhabited largely by a foreign element.

(b) 1. What places or neighborhoods in New York City should, in your opinion, be given special attention by Patrolwomen after a large fleet of U. S. warships has returned to this city following a long cruise? Give your reasons.

2. What special precautions or measures should, in your opinion, be taken by the women's branch of the Police Department in connection with the observance of Mardi Gras Week at Coney Island?

10. State fully what you, as a Patrolwoman, would do

(a) On seeing a man pick flowers from a

decorative flower bed in Central Park.

(b) On being assigned to investigate a complaint alleging immoral conditions in a certain commercial dance hall.

(c) On being sent to find out what you can concerning the alleged use of narcotics by some children attending a certain public school.

(d) If you saw a public taxicab driver drive his car unoccupied slowly along the curbstone and talking all the while to a nicely dressed young lady pedestrian who ignores the man entirely.

The importance of filling the position of policewoman through the formality of civil service examinations cannot be stressed too strongly. While appointment without examination is at times an excellent means of securing the right person for the right job, it carries with it the dangers of politics and personal favoritism, both of which have no place in the policewoman's sphere.

It is not uncommon, where an appointment system maintains, to find that the widows, wives and daughters of policemen are given a certain preference. There is a great deal of wisdom and justice in this, although without doubt should these same appointees be obliged to pass an examination, they would probably make a good showing.? This in fact, was the case in the first New York City examination when eight widows of policemen killed in the performance of their duty, succeeded in making the list creditably.

Although the womenfolks of a policeman's family are peculiarly well fitted to carry on his work, in recruiting women for the profession, they alone do not stand out as the only groups from which to draw for a supply. From the professional point of view, nurses, teachers, social workers, business women and women with industrial experience are particularly sought as likely material for the making of excellent policewomen. Occasionally a sensible motherly woman with no other experience than that of having raised a family makes one of the finest sort of protective officers.

So much depends upon the personality and disposition of the woman herself, regardless of her training and experience. It is so essential that she truly desires to serve, that she likes people and sincerely wishes to help them, that she possesses tact and judgment so that, in helping, she may act wisely at all times.

Any woman who is called upon to deal with young people, especially girls of adolescent age, should look well; this includes good personal appearance and good plain clothes. In befriending and guiding the wayward girl the policewoman often becomes a model. Moreover her quickest appeal is not one of words but of example.

Recently in New York City a young girl was manicuring the nails of a policewoman who believes in looking her best at all times, "I know you"—she ventured, after a few minutes, "I have seen your pictures in the paper and I have seen you dancing. You're not like the dowdy old woman that called us all sorts of names last Sunday at the beach because we didn't have our stockings on. Gee! she was a sight herself. What does she know about what a girl should wear these days anyway?"

Unfortunately there are some policewomen who do not know these things and have no understanding of the problems they have been called upon to handle nor the proper way of handling them. They are, however, in the minority, for most policewomen are modern women who accept the modern views of things and work out their problems in both a sympathetic and scientific way.

So far only the demands upon the woman who would undertake police work have been mentioned. If one must be all of these things, women will ask: What is the purpose? What is the return?

Standards

If a woman is really fitted to be a police-woman and wants to be one, the field is open to her; every opportunity is offered. As a profession for women, policewomanship carries with it many advantages. It is new work for women, which means that there is as yet no overcrowding and a chance for a woman with ideas and initiative to do constructive, pioneer work—to make history in fact. Fifty years ago the profession of trained nursing was as new as policewomanship is today. Then because the need of trained attendants for the sick in hospitals asserted itself, the Bellevue School of Nurses was started with just a handful of women. In fifty years that profession has become a foremost profession for women.

The offender against society is the sick man of today and the institution of policewomen to look after these sick people is as great and hopeful an enterprise as was the beginning of the profession of trained nurse. Fifty years from now—a brief space of time—will

find the profession of policewoman as well
standardized, universal and necessary as is the
work of the trained nurse today.

The fact that police work is a field of service
should appeal to women, for generally a woman desires to be of some use, to do some good.

Furthermore the work has in it an element
of excitement and change and therein differs
from the ordinary routine job a woman so
often accepts and remains in because she must
work and keep her position once she gets one.

Economically the position of policewoman
is attractive. In small towns the minimum
salary·is $1,000 or less, but in the larger cities
the minimum often approaches $2,500, while
it is prophesied that the maximum will some
day be $3,000. There is always opportunity
for advancement through promotion carrying
with it an increase in pay. Vacation, sick
leave, medical attention and a pension are
factors not to be overlooked. A college woman who has always commanded a good salary
recently declared that her advice to any young

woman choosing a profession would be to follow one that carried with it a provision for old age. The job of policewoman with its pension has this benefit.

In thinking of policewomen care must be taken not to confuse them with police matrons and probation officers. A policewoman performs a service different from either and holds her unique position in a Police Department. Then too, standards of all three positions vary. To have been a good police matron, for instance, does not especially qualify one to be a good policewoman, although there have been cases in which police matrons have attained the position of policewoman and rendered good service as such.

All told there are today some mighty good policewomen, more are needed* and more are wanted—so it behooves those who possess the qualifications to join the forces and help maintain the high standards that make the position worthy of women.

---

*Recently at a large gathering of representative European women it was declared that for every one hundred policemen there should be one policewoman. This seems a fair ratio.

ORGANIZATION

CHAPTER III

ORGANIZATION

"NOW that we've got policewomen, what are we going to do with them?" is the question asked by many an earnest chief of police when brought face to face with the problem of assigning women to police duty. Judging from the procedure that has been followed in working out a policewoman policy, there are three different answers to this question. Some cities, giving little thought to the matter, simply say: "Let them do the same work that the men are doing and become an integral part of the force. We've got to have them because it's a fad, but we're not going to bother with them much nor let them bother us. They'll soon get tired of their job or be swallowed up by the system anyway." This is what usually happens.

The answers of other cities show far more foresight. They say: "We need policewomen to handle some of our problems. They are particularly helpful in cases where children, girls and women are involved. We do not believe in giving them absolute jurisdiction over these matters as yet but we will do everything we can to make it possible for them to cooperate with the men of the force." This is a fair compromise and under such a system it is possible for policewomen to prove their worth.

The third answer is by far the best. It is this: "To do the most effective police work, policewomen must be organized as a unit to carry on their work. Give them full sway in their own particular field. Provide a Woman's Bureau with an able woman leader in charge and let them put the house in order." It is then that we have the finest work that policewomen can do.

Organization

In establishing a Woman's Bureau, it is important that a woman direct the program, but that she in turn be responsible to a superior officer of wider experience, preferably the Chief of Police or Commissioner, as such officer is called in so many large cities. A few cities have tried the experiment of having a woman Deputy Police Commissioner. So far this experiment seems to have failed but that does not prove that such a policy is not a good one. Although circumstances determine somewhat its success or failure, the significant factor is the woman herself. Some day some woman, by her ability, tact and personality will, if given the opportunity, make the position of Woman Deputy Police Commissioner a lasting tradition. Until that day it is sufficient that the pilots of policewomen be dubbed directors providing they truly carry on a Woman's Program.

When the first Women's Precinct was established in New York City a comprehensive program of work for women was drafted. It may resemble the programs of other cities, which only goes to show there is nothing new under the sun and people thinking along the same lines often arrive at the same conclusions.

This plan could be adopted without modifications to serve as a complete guide for the work of policewomen in any town, city or country. It could also be simplified to meet the needs of a small staff of workers. One woman alone could inject into her work all the ideas and principles that the program covers.

Policewomen's work should include three departments of activity: *Information and Aid, Detention* and *Education.* As each of these subjects will be treated in other chapters, a bare outline will suffice at this point.

A Woman's Program

I. *Information and Aid*

    A. Bureau of Information.

        A service bureau for women desir-

ing information and help in matters
where the police may act and serve.
B. Bureau of Protection and Prevention.
For the investigation and improvement of conditions endangering the
lives and welfare of children, girls
and women. Would have supervision over patrol, detective and
social case work.
C. A Women's Branch of the Bureau
of Missing Persons.
For the locating of missing persons,
particularly runaway girls, parents
of abandoned babies and other cases
where children, girls and women are
concerned. The work of this bureau would merely supplement that
of the central branch.
D. Corrective and General Police
Work.
Covering the regular police duties
of making arrests, if necessary, se-

curing evidence in special cases, apprehending persons sought by the police, observing and reporting violations of the law, detecting crime, securing physical and mental examinations and handling the cases of women and girls at station houses and headquarters.

The keeping of records and the making of reports is also a part of the daily routine duties.

E. Personnel and Welfare Work.

Rendering emergency aid to Policemen's families in cases of illness or death; investigation of pension cases; assisting in the furthering of social and welfare activities of the whole organization.

II. *Detention*

To this branch of the organization belongs the supervision and temporary care of girls who have not been charged with any criminal offense, runaway girls who have been located and detained at the request of their parents and women who might be stranded.

III. *Education*

Includes the training of policewomen and an appeal to the public to arouse their interest in police affairs and secure their cooperation.

To develop so broad a program it is not necessary to have a large staff of women. In fact in the beginning a small group is more advisable because whatever work is done at first is a foundation for all that follows. Hence the building up of the organization should progress slowly step by step and proceed only as the workers are ready for it. One cannot become a policewoman overnight. A year is a more reasonable period. Many policewomen will remember how long a time elapsed before they actually began to function as policewomen. The formative period is not wasted time, it is then that one should study and observe and strive to absorb the meaning and purpose of the vast organization that has called the policewoman into being. In these days one can find no better model, no better teacher than some faithful policeman who has devoted his life to the service. Every one is not fortunate enough to come under the tutelage of a type who welcomes women as friends and colleagues, but there are lessons to learn from watching any of these men at their work even though they do not consciously offer to play the part of pedagogue.

Women police, no matter how splendidly they are organized will never attain their ideal of service unless they cooperate wholeheartedly with the men of the force. Women have their own field, their own ideals and their own methods, but the service that they seek to render does not differ from that of the men. All rank alike, for it is all for the great good of mankind, a service of safety and protection of human beings.

EDUCATING POLICEWOMEN

CHAPTER IV

EDUCATING POLICEWOMEN

FOR many kinds of police work it is important that there be policewomen, but of greater importance is the systematic training of those who join the ranks in this capacity, so that the work once undertaken may be done well.

The pioneer policewomen were obliged to educate themselves to a large extent, learning police methods and routine chiefly through observation and bitter experience. To learn to do by doing is a sound pedagogical principle, but a combination of theory and practice in any educational scheme is always more direct and expedient. Hence the ideal system of teaching women policewomanship is to establish in connection with the actual field work, a training school where a short, intensive course along practical lines may be given to all beginners, and advance, continuation courses, aiming towards promotion, to those who have been longer in the service. It is essential that any city or town today employing women police for the first time provide some sort of preliminary police training no matter how otherwise well equipped the new appointees may be. This is the present policy of the New York Police Department. For one month during her probationary period every woman appointed attends a school the curriculum of which aims to teach her the fundamentals of a policewoman's job.

When a training school was contemplated in connection with the Women's Precinct, the aim and scope of the work was even broader. The course mapped out at that time was designed; First: To further train the women in the Police Department in policewomanship. Second: To train women recruits in police work. Third: To educate the public in

matters pertaining to the Police Department,
particularly those in which women, girls and
children are concerned. Fourth: To serve
as a model school in women police work and
thereby be a means of standardizing methods
used by policewomen. The program was
never fully carried out, but should New York
City or any other municipality ever adopt it,
the result would be a new era in the development of the usefulness and service of policewomen.

The course of study necessary to carry out
so comprehensive a plan could be followed
completely or be modified to meet the particular needs of a community or a given group
of workers. The subjects of the curriculum
planned may be classified as follows: 1.
Physical, including courses in Physical Training; Ju-Jutsu; Public Health and Sanitation;
Sex Hygiene; First Aid. 2. *Routine,* with
courses in Rules and Regulations; Deport-
ment and Discipline; Court Procedure; Report Making. 3. *Field Work,* covering

courses in Patrol and Observation; Social
Case Work; Information regarding the City.
4. *Theory,* embracing courses in Crimes Relating to Women and Children; Arrest; Penal
Code and City Ordinances regarding Children; Narcotics; Places of Public Amusement
and Public Morals; Fingerprinting and Personal Identification; Evidence and Psychology.

Such a course of study would naturally appeal only to those engaged in the work or woman seeking to enter the profession. For
these people there would be three possible
grades: 1. Student Classes; 2. Rookie Classes; 3. Advanced Classes for Policewomen.

The education of the public would be a
phase of the school's activity quite distinct
from the regular courses offered and would
consist largely of popular lectures and public
forums, to inform people of conditions, arouse
their interest in improving them and enlist
their cooperation to prevent crime.

In conducting a Police Department School

it is well, in so far as is possible, to recruit the teaching staff from among the more talented and experienced men in the service. This applies equally to a training school for policewomen. Many of the courses could be given by the more experienced women officers who have been engaged in the work for some time, others could be taught by the Department's experts in the particular subject required. Certain courses, such as one in First Aid, for instance, might be better handled by an outside organization like the Red Cross which specializes in that field. In a large city the many colleges offer the identical courses that the curriculum would call for and by arrangement these could be given to the students of the training school. The students of today would be the teachers of tomorrow, so eventually the school would become a distinct and important part of the women's branch of the organization.

Preparation for civil service examinations, promotion and the attaining of knowledge necessary to make one an expert in a subject would be contributory factors towards making the school a success and provide the incentives that all students require.

Should such training schools for policewomen become realities, it would not be long before certain definite standards as to the work of women in this field would be fixed, so that the principles and purposes underlying policewomen's service would become as well established and generally accepted as those followed by policemen. This would dignify the profession of Policewoman, attract to it the best type of worker and establish a closer bond of union between policewomen all over the world.

We need police department schools for the training of policewomen as greatly as we need the services of women police, for education is the keynote of effective preventive and protective police work which is the goal of the policewoman.

A WOMEN'S PRECINCT

CHAPTER V

A WOMEN'S PRECINCT

IN THE Spring of 1921, there was inaugurated in the City of New York a Women's Precinct. This novel institution, originated by a women and designed exclusively for the use of women was the first of its kind in that City. In fact probably nothing like it had ever before been featured in police administrations throughout the world.

Aside from the novelty of the idea, which caused the newspapers to give it wide publicity, the beginning of the first Women's Precinct is interesting because it marks a crisis in the history of policewomen's endeavors.

The building from which the Women's Precinct evolved was an old station house located in New York's notorious Hell's Kitchen.   It had long been abandoned by the men as a "dingy, dirty rat hole." This exactly describes the condition of the place before the women got in and began to clean it up. First the rat holes were stuffed, then followed a thorough scrubbing with soap and water, next came painters and carpenters who renovated the building from top to bottom and finally one of the policewomen with the assistance of several public spirited lay women completed the miracle by artistically furnishing and decorating. Indeed when all was finished it looked more like a charming club house for girls than an old time police station. The attractive reading room and comfortable dormitory contrasted strangely with the narrow, dark cells that were formerly used as a detention prison for women and which were retained as a part of the plant merely as a relic of another age.

The idea behind all this unusual transformation is the very essence of the principles for which the modern policewoman should stand. In removing from the Women's Precinct all the earmarks of a regular police station it at once became a center where a woman could seek information, advice or aid from those of her own sex without fear of being subjected to the grim atmosphere of the average police desk. The red geraniums in the window boxes would attract the attention of a woman even before the large letters spelling "Women's Precinct" caught her eye. Once over the threshold, the worried mother or weary, runaway girl could find the help, understanding and protection that only a motherly policewoman can give.

Not alone did the Women's Precinct itself extend an invitation to women, girls and children in distress and trouble, but the Commissioner of Police sent thousands of formal printed notices to the general public appraising them of the purposes of the new institution and urging them to take advantage of its facilities. "The Women's Precinct at 434 West 37th Street," the invitation read, "is always

[59]

open for inspection by those who are interested in the activities of women in police work. We welcome you as a visitor or as a volunteer worker.

"Under the direction of Patrolwoman Mary E. Hamilton a broad program for preventive and protective work with children, girls and women is being carried on.

"This program embraces three splendid activities: Information Bureau for Women; City's Guest Dormitory for Moral Girls and Training School for Policewomen. It is also a Civic Educational centre for public spirited citizens and civic welfare groups.

"The building has been thoroughly renovated and especially equipped for its use and will doubtless serve as a model for other Women's Precincts.

"We want you to share in this new service and broad educational work and help us make the Women's Precinct of the Police Department* one of the biggest movements for the

*See chapter on organization.

betterment of human conditions that the City of New York has ever undertaken."

An editorial comment in the New York Herald fairly describes this first police station for women:

"The ideal thing would be to keep women away from police stations altogether, to keep out of women's lives all that police interference represents. Unhappily, this degree of perfection has not yet been reached by any community, however civilized. The next best thing, unquestionably, is to make women's contact with the police as little demoralizing to them as possible.

It is therefore wise and humane to open a special police station for women and to place its administration, so far as is possible, in the hands of women. Thus the rigors of detention may be softened to many unfortunates, and to those who have gone astray whatever remains of self-respect may be saved as a foundation for betterment.

Advantage has been taken of an abandoned station house far over on the West Side of the city to get the idea, which has long been talked of, put into operation in practical form. The location is very unsuitable, the house is old fashioned, but perhaps it is well to get going on any terms. If the institution proves as useful as its advocates hope, it will not be difficult in a year or two to get a central site and a modern building. The present place will do for experimental purposes.

Two women of experience are in charge of the work. They have a large sized programme in their minds. First of all comes the decent treatment of women prisoners; above all things, the segregation of the merely

The Policewoman

wayward, the almost innocent from the contagious influence of these hardened in vice and crime. This result alone, if effectually attained, would justify the whole enterprise. But there is also in view a service bureau for women who desire information or help in matters of police jurisdiction, such as treatment of wayward girls, hunting for lost relatives and preliminary steps to settle domestic friction.

Besides, a temporary place of detention for girls who are not criminals, but who are held for preventive purposes or as witnesses, is contemplated. Plainly this is a great need and the plan to protect them by nurses, physicians and teachers while under restraint is to eliminate the present evils of idleness and promiscuous companionship in such cases. Finally, Mrs. Hamilton hopes to see a training school established for women who are to enter correctional and protective work as a career, as members of the police or the probation service.

The new undertaking is distinctly progressive, even though only an experiment. It is in the line of suppressing evil near the source and suppressing crime by diverting possible criminals from its pursuit. The tryout of the project will be watched with sympathetic interest not only by penologists but by all well disposed people."

In the history of policewomen's work the Women's Precinct as it originated and developed stands out both as an achievement and as an ideal unfulfilled. Few know how much thought and labor were expended in order to make such an institution possible. The enthusiasm of the city officials and their guests at the formal opening seemed to assume a fulfillment of all the ideals that the institution represented to its originator. Here was an ideal place in which to carry on a wonderful program for women. Every feature of the Women's Precinct represented a vital phase of the kind of police work that women could do. If any city wants to start their policewomen right they could do nothing better or finer than to provide as headquarters for them a similar plant. Such is the achievement, the fact that the first Women's Precinct will always be a model of correct policewomen housing and administration. Soon after its origin, more urgent policies prevented the Women's Precinct from functioning in accordance with the plan of its founder. With the transfer from the Women's Precinct of this person who knew how the program was to be developed because she had originated it and in whose mind it was still in somewhat of an embryo stage, the

[63]

institution necessarily became more or less of a routine complaint bureau, to which men and women alike were assigned. Hence it never became the great force that it could have been had it proceeded along the lines for which it was designed.

The first Women's Precinct has not existed in a woman's mind or, for a short time, in fact without avail. It is a stepping stone in police-women's work, a distant light that can be seen from a great distance on a dark road.

PATROL

CHAPTER VI

PATROL

PATROL work is probably one of the most difficult jobs that the policewoman encounters when she first assumes her duty of watching over the lives of the women, girls and children of any community, in order to protect them and prevent harm from reaching them. It is, however, one of the most important phases of women police service and requires endurance, tact, alertness, good, quick judgment and the ability to do the right thing speedily in any emergency situation.

When in 1919, Commissioner Richard E. Enright increased the force of policewomen in New York City, an article appeared in a New York paper entitled "Policewomen Needed Badly by Girls Here." The follow-

[67]

ing excerpt is the opinion of an ordinary policeman, "who," as the reporter said, "knows nothing of and cares nothing for bookish sociology, but who has been "pounding a pavement long enough to have two stripes on his coat sleeve." He said:

"You ought to write something that will reach the mothers; something that will put them wise to what their kid daughters are doing. The younger they are, down to about thirteen, the worse they seem to be. They are afraid of no cops. They are afraid of nobody. A couple of days ago, about eleven at night, I saw four fellows coming toward the park fence here with two girls, each about fourteen. I stopped them. I told them they ought to be home, and they turned as if to go away.

"A little while later, while patrolling my beat through the park I saw a couple of the fellows, who were about eighteen years old, hoisting the same girls over the park fence. I gave chase. The girls ran in one direction and the boys in another. Those girls could run, but not so fast as the boys and I got them first. They were inclined to argue with me at first and only wilted when I told them that I was going to see them home. They pleaded and cried; they seemed to prefer even arrest; but I insisted, and marched them to their homes somewhere on Skillman Street.

"Their people were decent, hardworking folks, and as I left I could hear the girls' yells in the street. I don't think that I'll have much trouble with them any more. But there are lots of them coming into the park, very late at night, every night. I never saw so many bad kids. And they are bad. When you get through talking to them, you'd think they'd beat it home, but instead they sneak down one pathway of the park and hide along another. Kids, especially girls, were never like that in the old days."

It is this sort of patrolling that a woman can do better than a man and to this duty they are now usually assigned with good results.

In doing patrol duty the general policy of policewomen has been one of quiet, dignified, unobtrusive watchfulness. In not wearing a uniform, women officers have an advantage over the uniformed patrolmen, for they may mingle with the crowd without arousing suspicion and thereby detect conditions that would never exist while a bluecoat were in sight. If any one doubts this fact, recollect how quickly a good crap game can be completely disrupted when the "look-out" gives the fatal warning—"Cheese it—de Cop!"

With the usual small force of policewomen in any city it is impossible to cover every place where women and girls might congregate but with the excellent police protection that is provided by the male force, it is unquestionably not necessary to have a policewomen assigned to every post. There are certain places, however, that should be patrolled by policewomen because they are, so to speak, the very breeding places of crime and hence the logical domain over which the policewoman should have control in exercising her functions of preventing crime and protecting those who innocently or ignorantly might be drawn into the net. These danger centers are dance halls, cabarets, moving picture theatres, beaches, boats, railroad stations, taxicabs stands, parks and some streets. In fact all popular public places and resorts of commercial amusements in general.

Occasionally certain isolated spots constitute a greater source of danger than the gayer, more crowded places. Recently a community group in the Flatbush section of Brooklyn appealed to the New York Police Department for a policewoman to patrol a lonely stretch of road necessarily traversed by the children of the neighborhood each day on their way to school. Several flagrant sex crimes against very young children had prompted this action and upon careful investigation there was found to be a most urgent need for the particular kind of patrol service that a woman could render. Not only did the policewoman protect the danger center in the crisis, but she also took advantage of the opportunity presented by the joint appeal of parents to do some educational work among them, seeking to make them realize the great dangers that their children might be subjected to through careless neglect or ignorance and showing how through their cooperation it would be possible for the Police Department, especially through its force of women, to help avoid these dangers. In this way the patrolwoman became the neighborhood's friend and her services were gratefully received. This is the highest type of service a policewoman can render.

While patrol duty is often exciting, certain features make it more difficult for a woman than for a man. Patrol soon becomes monotonous, especially when nothing seems to happen. Then too the hours when patrol is necessary are generally unusual and continuous without relief. A great deal of this work must necessarily be done at night and for a woman to remain inconspicuously in any public place for any length of time, particularly at night is far more difficult than for a man. One cannot always say to the people who suspiciously watch—"I am a policewoman, I have a right to be here," for so many times to reveal one's identity frustrates one's usefulness completely.

There is one unfailing protection and that is the knowledge of the fact that the policeman on post stands ready to come to your aid. It is therefore, essential that you cooperate with him and make known your presence and mission. All of the patrol work done by the first policewomen of that large eastern city previously mentioned was impaired by the fact that they sought to work alone. An effective police force is like a great army—one person against the swift current of crime is of no account, but massed together, working side by side, the victory is half won.

Patrol work if done properly is not a mere routine job. It offers unlimited possibilities for policewomen to do real preventive work and places her in the midst of those most needing her protection. It also gives one an unusual opportunity to watch out for runaway girls and missing persons, to observe violations of the law and other irregularities affecting social welfare. Except in extreme cases the policewoman does not seek to arrest, the purpose of her patrol is to watch and warn and save as much as she can without antagonizing those she would help.

Patrol work is vitally important, but it is merely a phase of policewoman's work and to emphasize it unduly or assign women to that duty alone and nothing else is to lose sight of the real value of women's police service.

THE POLICEWOMAN AS A
DETECTIVE

CHAPTER VII

THE POLICEWOMAN AS A DETECTIVE

L ONG before any one thought about employing policewomen, women detectives
were engaged in the work of ferreting out
crime by applying their intuition, versatility
and natural feminine guile to cases whose
solution demanded these qualities rather than
the methods of the male sleuth. With the
advent of women police the detective field for
women at once broadened for detective work
became one of the most logical branches of the
service for which the sex is fitted.

It has been said that detectives are born not
made, and to do first class work along this line
one must have a peculiar aptitude for it.
This may account for the unusual detective
skill that is sometimes displayed by police-

women who have not specialized in the field. Training invariably reveals either talent or inability to follow the facinating trail, for although every policewoman is given an opportunity to obtain the knowledge and experience necessary to become a clever detective, all do not qualify for this particular kind of work; in fact to many women detective duty is actually distasteful.

When a regular official women's detective force was established in Lancashire, England, the Chief Constable tried out the women first in the clerical division as typists, stenographers, and card indexers. As he saw that he could trust them with confidential matters he promoted the brightest ones to the detective force.

One very clever American woman detective began her career as an office girl. While so employed she diligently studied the daily reports of the various operatives until finally she felt that she had mastered the technique of detectiveship sufficiently to warrant her ap-

---

plying for a regular position. She subsequently approached the head of a leading agency who interrogated her at length and seemed pleased and satisfied with her glib answers and broad knowledge. As the interview neared an end he suddenly asked, "What is roping?" She had never heard of the term, common as it is, but her quick wit saved her. "Mr. ——," she exclaimed, "you really don't want to ask me so simple a question, do you?" They both laughed and the job was hers.

When conservative Scotland Yard announced that women were a decided value to its detective force and pointed out that in several important murder cases it was they who secured information which proved the most important clues, the policewoman detective appeared in a new light. This was official recognition. Sir Neville Macready, until lately head of the metropolitan police in London, declared that all types of women detectives were needed; those who could put on evening clothes and mix with people at social events, as well as women who could don the make up of a woman of doubtful morals and frequent the underworld on an equal footing with the men and women hiding there from the law.

Aside from the big criminal cases, a woman detective in any city can do some excellent sleuth work in the course of her daily duties. A few actual cases will illustrate how varied one's assignments may be. A woman detective can answer advertisements for help wanted and trap the men who attempt to insult her as they have other girls before any complaints were made. She can ensnare "mashers" who lie in wait for more innocent victims. Under the guise of a woman's curiosity she can approach fortune tellers and other soothsayers who ply their art regardless of the law. Her sex also makes her the unsuspected patient of the abortionist. With her knowledge of materials and familiarity with styles, she can easily identify stolen goods, particularly if they be women's clothes. Valuable service can likewise be rendered by her in detecting shoplifters. In matters of prohibition enforcement women have even proven themselves to be adept in buying a drink, thereby procuring the necessary evidence to convict the proprietors of cabarets for violations of the law. These simple tasks could be enumerated at length before every phase of detective work for women could be completely covered.

It is not an uncommon practice for the wives of some detectives to assist in cases where the presence of a woman strengthens the search, hence many of the policemen's widows who become policewomen bring with them into their work a wealth of detective knowledge and skill.

Women desiring to become proficient detectives must remember that crimes are solved by intelligence, hard work and, in the opinion of a learned authority, because of a certain amount of luck. In the solution of a crime

[81]

one must proceed slowly and methodically. Some of the best detectives write down everything they observe step by step. It is well to remember these few simple rules: Take photographs of the scene of the crime, whatever and wherever it may be. Save the fingerprints, which necessitates preserving every article that the criminal may have touched. Big crimes have been reconstructed from an invisible thumb print on a bit of wallpaper. Do not allow the neighbors or sightseers to inspect the premises until a thorough examination has been made by you. Move in a circle from the scene of a crime, noting footsteps, wagon tracks and similar traces. Question every one living in the vicinity, gradually widening your circle. Ask questions, but never answer them. Listen but do not talk.

No system is infallible; each case must be treated according to the circumstances which surround it. To be able to adapt oneself to the case at hand and put into it every faculty one possesses is a test of a policewoman's talent as a detective.

The Policewoman as a Detective

A detective must observe keenly and develop a good memory. She must be a student of psychology, understanding the mental impulses, emotions and motives of normal, sane and criminal persons.

Indentification is another subject to be mastered; not only indentification by means of finger prints, but the recognition of persons from features, posture, personal habits, gait and gestures.

The art of cross examination should be learned if a detective expects to secure by questioning proper deductions. Often a certain type of question will result in an emotional reaction that will clearly indicate the innocence or guilt of a suspect. Trailing and disguise, so vital in the detective game come only with practice and experience.

Abraham Lincoln was a great lawyer and his success at the bar was largely attributed to the fact that before he worked up his own side of a case, he first thoroughly studied his opponent's position. A detective can practically do the same thing by approaching the crime from the criminal's point of view. To do so it is necessary to know the methods that criminals use in committing crime. The accidental criminal works one way, the habitual violator of the law another, while the unfortunate moron, low grade mental defective or insane type, whose heredity rather than environment is responsible for his act, operates wholly unlike either.

A detective's life is exciting and variable; theirs is a service that could not be dispensed with by any highly civilized community for crime seems to be a waste product of a complex social organization and an ever present problem. A woman specializing in this field must remember that in her work she lives many lives and impersonates many characters. She may meet people whose friendship she would like to hold but to do so often endangers her professionally. It is often a lonely job. A young woman detective, posing as an heiress at a fashionable summer resort met

[84]

a man whom she liked very much. A few weeks later she found herself dusting his room as she was acting in the capacity of maid in a city hotel. He thought that he recognized her and called her by name, but she had to tell him roughly to "go on" and "quit kiddin'."

Detectiveship is a profession that should attract women of education because it requires a trained mind to cope with the modern criminal. It is a very likely profession for the college graduate. Before choosing it, however, a girl should measure her capabilities and temperament and weigh carefully the opportunities and disadvantages that the job carries with it.

THE RUNAWAY

CHAPTER VIII

THE RUNAWAY

WHAT causes a boy or girl to leave home and run away? There are many answers to this question and unless a policewoman knows all of them, she is not fully equipped to cope with one of her biggest problems—The Runaway.

When it is remembered that America was founded by a group of people who broke away from traditions distasteful to them and braved the severest hardships for an ideal and a belief, it is easy to understand the spirit that causes the boys and girls of today to strike out for themselves. Then too, so many of them have for their heritage the courage of their immigrant ancestors who came to America to escape oppression and win for themselves fame, fortune and freedom. And then above all is youth's eternal longing for Adventure.

These inherent tendencies are for the most part remote causes of wanderlust, the immediate reasons range from the sublime to the ridiculous.

A boy of twelve ran away from his home in New Haven, Connecticut, and came to New York City to see the Woolworth Building. A New Jersey lad, eleven years of age, left his home for the thirty-fifth time, each time visiting a different section of New York City. When he was last picked up, while wandering around the lower East Side, he explained that he just couldn't stay away from New York. Another six year old boy covered most of Brooklyn, Manhattan and Philadelphia in the course of forty-five runaway trips. Both boys and girls from city and country have been known to start out on world hikes. This is Wanderlust in an extreme form.

Many children run away to escape unhappy home conditions. Fear of punishment and parental wrath often compel them to flee when it would be far better for them to remain at home and take their medicine. It is these children who, out of desperation, easily become the prey of vicious persons, because they have no definite purpose in mind when they start out and welcome suggestions from suave strangers.

Several years ago a young girl left her home in a small town after a quarrel with her parents over a trifling matter and came to New York City. She rented the first furnished room she happened to see, little realizing that she was walking into a house of prostitution. The first night she was there, the house was raided by the police and although she was actually only a lodger, she was arrested and brought into court, because the circumstances seemed to indicate that she was an inmate of the house being held in reserve.

The injustice of her situation so incensed the young woman that she stubbornly refused to give any information regarding herself.

Had not a policewoman been called who succeeded in gaining her confidence, that innocent girl would have been sent to prison with the record of a prostitute against her for all time.

Through the kindly intervention of the Judge, a reconciliation between her and her family was brought about and she returned home, a much wiser girl for her terrible experience.

Some runaway girls are less fortunate. Recently a young woman of seventeen was found murdered. She proved to be the runaway daughter of a father who was too strict.

Too many times a father's strictness figures prominently among the girls' reasons for running away. A typical tragic case is one in which the father takes every cent his daughter earns, allowing her no spending money except ten cents for carfare each day and perhaps fifteen cents for lunch. When she returns home from work, she is relegated to the kitchen; a moving picture show would completely disrupt her morale and lower her standard of working efficiency. Young people, especially young men, are entirely out of the question.

Finally rebelling against such treatment the girl deserts the parental roof much to the grief and consternation of her parents. If she has sense, and luck favors her, she may become self supporting. Many runaway girls, making a sincere and honest effort to support themselves, succeed in doing so. Others ignorantly brave, with little or no money and no idea of what to do, once they are free from the severe parental restrictions, soon become discouraged, fall in with bad companions and gradually drift into bad ways or an easy mode of life.

Taking a girl's hard earned money and curbing her high-spirited, fun-loving craving for innocent pleasures are mild phases of parental control compared with the cases in which a father's brutality is the driving force that compels the girl to assert her independence and go forth to live her own life.

In the following newspaper query for advice the plaint of the girl struggling against unbearable home conditions is sounded:

Dear Mary Judge:

I am a girl of eighteen. I'm told that I am beautiful, so my parents think in order that I shan't be vain they must treat me as humiliatingly as possible. I live out in the country, am one of six children, do almost all the work of the house, and have no friends.

I feel like I am in chains, and I long to get away and see the world. I'd like to be an actress, but I don't dare to speak of it at home. I am not allowed even to go for a stroll with one girl companion for fear I will meet a boy and speak with him.

There is a certain young man who comes often to the house and wants to marry me. I do not care for him. I told my parents I wouldn't marry any man until I had been out in the world and seen a little of life.

They taunt me with this remark. Sometimes I think they will drive me to marry him to get away, and yet I am sure my parents love me in their peculiar way. Think of it, I have been to a movie only a few times in my life.

I don't care if I never marry if I can secure freedom. But I don't want to disgrace my family. They are beginning to nag me about having no suitors. I don't want them, the ones I see.

And how can I meet others, when I never have opportunity to go out?

MARION.

The Runaway

"Unhappy little Marion, longing for freedom, and life, and the stage, and education, and still clinging a bit to home, besides! Yours is a problem, but it is one many other girls your age share with you.

You are eighteen now. No one outside your family can decide things for you. If you feel the urge to go away and work for a living, and have the courage to do it; to face hardships (especially if you persist in trying for the stage), then leave your home for a while.

The Y. W. C. A. will give you assistance if you have enough money to support yourself until you get a position.

But if you have no money, and your parents refuse to help you get started in some outside work, then you must be content to remain at home and make the best of it."

The tragedy of the lost girl or boy is a tragedy of misunderstanding, a conflict between the conservative point of view of a past generation and the eager, liberal outlook of a modern age. Yet the blame for runaway sons and daughters cannot be placed entirely upon the parents for frequently they are "more sinned against than sinning." Sometimes the motives for running away could be swerved in another direction through a proper educational impetus. We can point out to the fathers and mothers their responsibility in the matter, when the mistake is theirs, but when the children are in error, we must correct an educational system or perhaps mend a flaw in the fabric of society itself in order to solve the problem.

Every year thousands of runaway boys and girls, the majority being girls, are picked up in the streets of New York. Without doubt as many leave this city to seek fame as come to it. Stage struck girls and those who are movie mad are lured away from home to New Orleans, San Francisco, Baltimore and other cities with little or nothing in their pockets except a railroad ticket supplied to them by a theatrical agency.

Recently a group of twelve girls, only two of whom were over sixteen, were detained as they were about to board a train for New Orleans to dance in a cabaret. One of the young aspirants, a girl fifteen years of age, had run away from home because she was tired of school. Her world possessions consisted of seventy dollars and her mother's fur coat.

Had these girls been allowed to leave the
city, they would probably have dropped out
of sight. It has been estimated that within a
single year, sixty-five thousand girls disappear
in the United States without leaving a trace.

In this particular case the girls had no con-
tracts, practically no money, no means of returning to their homes if they did not like
their work and since they were not trained to
do professional dancing, they would probably meet only gross failure and be obliged
to face all of these problems. Only by chance
on the eve of their departure was the group
brought to the attention of a policewoman.
It was possible to save them from their folly,
but how many other untrained girls who seek
stage careers out of town are never reached!
It is they who become the problems of policewomen in other cities, for just as New York
is obliged to recover, clean and care for that
appalling army of girls and boys who are
found on the streets, in subways, comfort sta-

tions and cheap lodging houses, so other communities are similarly burdened.

Little children usually run away between the ages of three and six in pursuit of some object that interests them. A youngster three years old walked seven miles to go to school. That was his greatest desire. Another baby parked his kiddie-car at a subway entrance in the suburbs of New York and travelled to the center of the city's gay life—Forty-second Street and Broadway. Once provided with an interest greater than the one which sends him forth, the child of tender years will play contentedly at home. In the case of the young child, running away can be cured by intelligent handling. Once it is discovered why the child runs away it is easy to substitute a more wholesome impulse for the runaway habit. Whipping a child will never prevent his running away again.

Another runaway age is the adolescent period. A boy or girl is apt to go to extremes at this time, emotionally and mentally.

The Runaway

The motives which prompt youths to run away; hurt feelings, desire to be alone, rebellion against authority, boredom, love of adventure and a desire to see the world, all indicate a mental, emotional and physical awakening. The adolescent is an idealist. His purposes are for the most part altruistic. Few boys and girls leave home because they have gone wrong. In most cases it is frank impulse or innocent desire that causes a boy to run away to sea or join the army, while the bright lights of Broadway, the jazz of the dance halls, automobiles and fine clothes attract the girl, because they represent her ideal of the beautiful. She makes an idol of a famous actress and strives to mold her life accordingly. In her dreams, she sees herself in this role. To attain her ideal more completely she starts out, for did not the popular star begin her career as a poor girl? She reaches a destination, she may be beaten for the time being, but in her heart she always feels that success is just around the corner. If her goal is New York, and there the bubble bursts, she is confident that Chicago holds for her the fulfillment of her dearest hopes. When Chicago disappoints her, she sees success just ahead for her in San Francisco.

To break down the faith of the adolescent is a hopeless task. Only through appealing to the emotions, by supplying the boy or girl with some wholesome means of self expression can thèse forces be deflected from a foolish course to a wise and wholesome one.

This is the policewoman's task when she is confronted with the runaway girl or boy. There is no set formula for handling a runaway case, for each one varies with the individual and the circumstances.

If the child is tired, dirty and hungry—attend to his physical needs first. The psychological effect of being rested, clean and satisfied often changes the whole outlook of a person. A problem that hovers over us at night seems stupendous, but let the morning sunshine reach it and it sinks into insignificant littleness.

The important thing before attempting to do anything about the case, is to get the story —the whole truth and nothing but the truth. Find out what's wrong with the runaway, the runaway's parents and home. Be fair, firm, kindly and understanding. Gain the confidence of the narrator and never abuse that sacred trust.

You may find that all the boy needs is to be shown the sights of the city—if so, be his guide for a day. He will then go home satisfied and won't want to run away again.

Sometimes an appeal to the emotions will win the heart of the runaway,—a white rose, a pathetic magazine story have been known to send a girl home repentant.

If the facts of the case indicate that the fault lies with the parents, the home, the environment, it is useless to return the boy or girl until a complete readjustment has been accomplished. This is not easily done; it requires great tact and wisdom on the part of the policewoman.

When you have won a girl or boy and see a father or mother rush to greet the prodigal with upraised hand, it is better to delay the return until the parent also experiences a change of heart.

Remember that the runaway has violated no law and in being detained to await the arrival of relatives or friends should not be imprisoned. Detention quarters for runaways should be attractive and wholesome, designed to inspire hope and confidence and restore the wanderer to a more normal state of mind and course of action.

In reclaiming runaways, policewomen are saving children whose brightness and bravery will serve society in a better way at some future time.

DETENTION

CHAPTER IX

DETENTION

EVERY one knows that good fruit quickly decays when it remains for any time in a basket with rotten fruit. The same principle applies when unconvicted girls and women, who may or may not be guilty of any crime and if guilty are first offenders, are incarcerated in the same place with hardened criminals of maturer years.

Since it is the police, who, for various reasons first detain these people, it is the responsibility of the policewoman to maintain proper detention facilities for girls and women, because it is they who are their special wards.

The conditions of detention in New York City illustrate the problem as it is apt to exist in any city. The Charter of the City of New York provides that persons detained as witnesses or persons detained for trial and examination shall not be put in the same room with convicts under sentence; that minors shall not be put or kept in the same room with adult persons and that a woman detained in any county jail or penitentiary upon a criminal charge or as a convict under sentence shall not be kept in the same room with a man; and if detained on civil process or for contempt or as a witness, she shall not be put or kept in the same room with a man except her husband.

For the detention and confinement of women under arrest in New York City, such station houses are used as are assigned by the Police Commissioner. It is the duty of the Police Commissioner to provide sufficient accommodations for women held under arrest to keep them separate and apart from the cells, corridors and apartments provided for males under arrest and to so arrange each station house that no communication can be had be-

tween the men and women therein confined
except with the consent of the matron or officer in command of said station house.

Whenever a woman is arrested and taken
to a police station to which a matron is attached, it is the duty of the officer in command to summon the matron, who remains in
attendance so long as the woman is detained
there. If no matron is on duty at the precinct
in the district where the woman was appre-
hended, the woman prisoner must be taken
directly to the station house which has been
assigned by the Commissioner to receive women. Minors may be transferred to the cus-
tody of a society whose purpose it is to care
for children. Under a central, municipal
detention house system all women and children could be taken directly there without un-
dergoing the usual police station desk inquiry.

Pending the arraignment or trial of prisoners, adequate provisions must be made for the
separation of female from male prisoners and
youthful and less hardened offenders from the
older and more hardened ones of the same sex.

According to the law, a house of detention where women may be detained before and after being heard, must be convenient to the court for women, for it is important that convicted persons be detained where they are readily accessible to the various individuals and agencies investigating their cases, such as the Board of Health, Probation officers, counsel, relatives and friends.

Formerly women were kept overnight in police stations, but this practice has been practically abandoned and certain prisons, notably Jefferson Market Prison and Raymond Street Jail are now used as houses of detention for women. For runaways and women detained as material witnesses, it has been customary for the court to designate for this use certain private institutions such as Waverly House and The Florence Crittenton Home.

None of these detention facilities is ideal. Some of the institutions, not having been designed for the purpose, are inconvenient and inadequate. Then too, because there is no large central House of Detention under municipal administration an important public duty is necessarily delegated to private individuals with the result that the responsibility is scattered. Frequently girls who have been detained pending an investigation by the police have been unwittingly discharged from private houses of detention before the investigation has been completed and important police work is impeded.

Formerly the police were not well equipped to handle the problem of detention for women, but now that policewomen have joined the force, they are in a position to do this kind of work better than any extra-judicial body.

When the first Women's Precinct was established, detention quarters were provided there for unconvicted girls and women. This was a definite step in the right direction. Had the full program been carried out at the Women's Precinct the problem of detention in New York City would have been greatly simplified,

[109]

because a large group, the innocent and un-convicted, would have been scientifically cared for in accordance with the most modern ideas.

The Women's Precinct, however, pointed out the great need for better detention in New York City. When it was no longer used for this purpose, the evils of the old system seemed even more flagrant. It was then decided to house all women prisoners in special deten-tion quarters on Welfare Island, an institu-tion far removed from the courts and general-ly inaccessible. Because of the difficulties of transportation and the numerous protests against a system that necessitated the con-tinuous transferring of prisoners to and from the courts at a great distance, the project failed and once again the city prisons and private institutions became the principal centers of detention.

The last move to improve detention con-ditions in New York City was made by the Board of Estimate through its appropriation of $750,000 to be used by the Commissioner of Correction in the construction of a Woman's Court and Detention Center. The institution remains to be developed.

Any city employing the services of policewomen should see that these officers supervise the detention of women, girls and children. We have policewomen to protect this group and prevent crime among them. Proper detention is one of the biggest preventive and protective measures that the policewoman has at her command.

The right kind of detention home should not be a prison. Prisons are factories of nonproduction and waste. It should be a home for the unfortunate, a hospital for the sick, a rehabilitation center for the discouraged and a vocational school for the unadjusted. To be sure, the population of such an institution is transient, but just as it does not take long to send a girl to the devil, so in an equally short space of time, she may be put on the right track. So much depends upon the personality of her advisors during this critical period, the character of her environment and the method of approach. Many a girl is saved by suggestion alone. The policewoman in a detention home must know how to say the right thing at the right time and in the right place. She must remember that every girl whether good or bad is a potential mother, and in her rests the hope of the next generation, for no civilization is greater than its mothers nor better than its children.

FINGERPRINTING AND
IDENTIFICATION

CHAPTER X

FINGERPRINTING AND IDENTIFICATION

FINGERPRINTING is a profession in which women easily excel for they are peculiarly well fitted to handle the great mass of detail involved in this useful and facinating art.

Since fingerprinting has become an important branch of police work, it is possible for the policewoman to enter the field and even become an expert, if she chooses to specialize in the subject.

For all policewomen to have a working knowledge of fingerprinting is absolutely necessary, because in that positive mark, the fingerprint, can be found the solution of so many problems against which the policewoman is laboring.

How simple would be the appalling situation of abandoned babies, were it possible to identify these unfortunate waifs by their tiny footprints. The opponents of universal fingerprinting should at least concede this point and favor the footprinting of all infants at birth, so that the tragedy of the innocent, unknown child, would be effaced forever.

In one day an average of nine deserted or murdered babies are reported in New York City. They are placed on roofs and doorsteps, left in hallways, comfort stations, telephone booths and ash cans, handed to small boys to mind by mothers who never return, sent to people in boxes, expensive shopping bags and suitcases; deserted in respectable hotels, day nurseries and churches. But by far the worst sort of abandonment is that in which a child is taken to an isolated spot and left to die of exposure, starvation and torture —the prey of flies, rats and other vermin.

There was a time in the social history of New York City when the good nuns of a famous foundling asylum placed a cradle outside of the institution, so that a mother driven to desperation could, unobserved, leave her baby in safe keeping. In seeking to remedy the evil of not knowing a child's pedigree, the custom was prohibited and now all the particulars regarding a child's parentage must become a matter of record before this institution will accept the charge.

This has not lessened the number of abandonments nor aided considerably in decreasing the rate of unidentified babies.

In New York State the maximum sentence on an abandonment charge is seven years. Most of the offenders are never brought to punishment, because the clues that might lead to an identification are meagre, if there are any at all.

Abandonment is a serious offense. On the face of it, it would seem as though no punishment could be severe enough for the woman who casts away her own flesh and blood. It is more heartless than murder.

Analyze the situation, examine the reasons that cause women to deliver their babies into the hands of Fate to live or die unknown and it must be admitted that the crime is largely the crime of society, shared by all alike.

The unmarried mother abandons her baby because she cannot face the scorn of family and friends, she cannot obtain work when she applies for it with a babe in her arms; even with money in her purse she is sometimes turned away from a respectable rooming house if she appears with a baby.

For lack of proper care during her confinement a woman sometimes becomes a physical wreck. In pain and terror or ignorance, she strives to get rid of that which seems to have caused her agony.

A mother, starving, because of society's failure to give her and her family a square economic deal leaves her baby on the doorstep of some one more fortunate than she. "Baby was privately baptized," she writes, "God, help the poor."

Fingerprinting and Identification

In many cases the man is the one who actually abandons the baby under the guise of placing it with some one for safe keeping. Invariably when the woman is the guilty one, mother instinct compels her to haunt the scene of her crime and sometimes she even appeals to the police to return her baby to her.

The policewoman cannot remedy these evils by a broad sweeping reform, although in a quiet way she may help to soften the attitude of society towards the unmarried mother and help in this to remove the unjust brand that is placed upon a child born out of wedlock.

Every policewoman can also work for the footprinting of babies at birth and thereby strive to lessen the tragedies of the abandoned child.

It seems strange that there should be an opposition to a system which so pointedly protects. To be sure, fingerprinting has unfortunately been too long associated in the minds of people with the criminal. The fingerprinting of a prisoner is really no different

[119]

than the photographing of him, yet we balk at fingerprinting and continue to have our pictures taken.

"Fingerprints," said the great naturalist, John Burroughs, "are the signature of nature on her handiwork, man." When this view is accepted and the good uses of fingerprinting realized, the fact that the police embody a fingerprint in a criminal record is a detail that interests us only as the Rogues Gallery does.

There have been numerous cases of mistaken identity of newborn babies in hospitals and the only infallible means of establishing a true identification is the registry of the footprints* of babies at birth together with the fingerprint of the mother. Such a record can be made on the back of the birth certificate and filed in the Bureau of Vital Statistics of the Department of Health. Not only would the baby mix-up be prevented for all time, but within a generation, these records would

*The footprint of the baby is used because a newborn infant closes its hands so tightly that a good fingerprint would be difficult to obtain.

constitute an infallible means of identification for every person in the country. There would be no more unknown dead. The thousands of tragedies that the Potter's Fields now hold would no longer be possible.

In order to understand fully the dangers of mistaken or doubtful identity of babies it is well to review a few of the more recent cases.

In a big city hospital a Jewish infant was given to an Italian mother, while the Italian child became a member of the other household. One of the children died before the mistake was discovered, and the bereaved mother will always feel that had she cared for her own baby its precious life might have been saved.

In the much discussed Rich case the mother declared that the doctor had told her that she had given birth to a boy. When a baby girl was handed to Mrs. Rich, she refused to accept it. The Riches thereupon brought suit against the hospital authorities charging that the babies were mixed and that they were given the child of another, while their offspring was discharged to some one else.

The court decided that the girl baby was undoubtedly the woman's child as shown by the record. That the doctor's statement that the baby was a boy was made to her at the time of her greatest suffering in order to soothe her, because she was so eager to give birth to a son.

The woman finally accepted the child, but declared that she would always be haunted by the idea that the child is not her own.

Only by adopting the system of footprinting children at birth can hospitals safely protect themselves against accidental confusion of babies, and a mother be absolutely sure that the baby she takes home to love and nuture *is* her own.

Some hospitals have been progressive enough to institute the idea of the footprinting of babies at birth and the fingerprinting of mothers even before a law exists compelling them to do so. The New York Nursery and

Child's Hospital at No. 161 West 61st Street, New York City has been foremost in the movement with an initial collection of six thousand babies' footprints.

Within a few minutes after birth, before the mother and child leave the operating room, the infallible record is made, first on the birth certificate, then on the hospital chart. Together with the footprint of the child appears the right index fingerprint of the mother. These prints cannot be separated and definitely establish the identification of the mother and child for all time. The birth certificate record is filed in the Bureau of Vital Statistics the hospital chart placed in a fireproof vault for safe-keeping.

At the present time the footprinting of babies at birth is wholly a voluntary matter. Not until there is a law making it as compulsory as the filing of a birth certificate will there be any universal acceptance of the system. Here is a cause worthy of the support of every thoughtful man, woman and child.

Aside from hospital mix-ups is the matter of the use of the fingerprint or footprint to identify the child who is kidnapped during early life. No hypothetical cases are needed to illustrate such a tragedy. It has stalked into several happy homes and is a situation that any father or mother might one day face —the mysterious disappearance of your baby —weeks elapsing—years passing by—then a clue and you brought face to face with a boy that might be your boy. But can you ever be sure that the child twelve years old is the self-same little fellow that was taken away from you in babyhood? There is only one positive means of identification—the foot or finger-print.

There is the old, sad case of Charlie Ross, the new, sad case of Lillian McKenzie and somewhere along through the years other kidnapped children stray. Bereaved parents still question—"Where is my child?" A greater and more difficult question to answer is "Who is my child?"

Ask yourself the question: "If my child were to disappear today, could I identify him eight years hence?"

There is only one sure way of knowing who your baby is now or in the future, and that is by having a record of the one made that time cannot efface—his finger or footprints.

A good many mysteries have centered around amnesia and aphasia cases. "Who am I?" moans a poor girl from a hospital cot. "Who is this man?" asks the newspapers in blazing headlines, while the picture of the lost man makes a mute appeal. These are only two typical cases from among a host of lost people.

Aside from their own suffering and the hardships they endure in adjusting themselves to the vague, new world in which they grope, is the agony of family and friends. Theirs is a worry that kills as surely as does any disease. So much money is spent nowadays to prevent disease that we cannot afford to overlook a preventive measure that will save human life by making impossible a mental strain which breaks down human efficiency. Fingerprint and register the record of a man and he will never undergo the horrible experience of not knowing who he is.

From the point of view of preventing worry, the identification of the dead is as necessary as the identification of the living. Without a system of fingerprinting, there are scores of people, victims of sudden death, accident and false play, who daily are relegated to unknown graves, simply because society has never provided a simple means whereby their identity could be established in emergencies.

For possible future identification, although no universal system of fingerprinting exists, every dead person should be fingerprinted. Such a record may be subsequently used to establish the fact of death to prevent insurance and other frauds. Then too, there may be recorded somewhere a fingerprint which corresponds to that of the unknown dead person and in this way his identity is fixed.

Fingerprinting and Identification

Thousands who die in great disasters could easily be identified by a small patch of skin* if only a fingerprint record existed. Fingerprinting and Identification, or Nothing and the Potter's Field—Which is better?

In spite of all the cases that show the need of a system of universal fingerprinting, there is much opposition to such a plan. These objections center mainly around the idea that universal fingerprinting would violate the personal rights of an individual. Frequently, for the greater good, a government, exercising its police power, limits the freedom of the individual to do as he pleases. Universal fingerprinting is undoubtedly a greater good measure.

Then too, it seems difficult for some people to dissociate criminal identification and personal identification. Fingerprinting to the unthinking man means only one thing, the

---

*With a fingerprint record a complete identification can be made by an examination of the skin pores. This is known as the science of poroscopy.

fingerprinting of criminals. He does not see in it a sane, simple and safe method of protecting millions of people.

The adoption of fingerprinting by the United States Post Office for the protection of its bank depositors and employees, its use in the United States Navy to safeguard against pay check forgeries and to identify every man in the service, a practical application of fingerprinting by Civil Service Commission, the sanction of the Courts in receiving fingerprints as signatures on documents instead of the familiar old "his (X) mark" together with the gradual recognition of fingerprinting as an invaluable aid in commercial matters, all help to overcome the prejudice that has grown up around fingerprinting in its association with the underworld.

Recently a prominent banker whose depositors include a large foreign population stated that upon hearing a lecture on fingerprinting he immediately installed a system in his bank. Today he has 125,000 depositors, all fingerprinted. Only by this means was it possible to eliminate the many frauds that resulted because of the fact that the signature or X of a depositor could be so easily forged, for most of these people were illiterate foreigners. Furthermore the information that they gave relevant to their personal history was known by their family and friends. Family and racial resemblance made it easy for another to impersonate the real depositor so the bank lost a great deal of money by paying it out to the wrong person before fingerprinting, the sure means of identification, was adopted. Fingerprints as signatures eliminate forgery in the banking business.

From September 1921 to June 1922, three clever forgers robbed fifty banks and trust companies in fifteen States to the amount of more than $100,000 by check writing operations. This represents only a small portion of such losses.

In seeking to remove the criminal stigma from fingerprinting the policewoman must not make the mistake of overlooking finger-printing in its application to the solution of crime. A single fingerprint has been known to convict a person of a crime, whereas the innocence of a person may be established by fingerprint evidence alone.

Once thirty-eight witnesses positively identified a suspect as being a certain person charged with swindling. When his fingerprints were compared with those of the real culprit, which were on record, it was found that they in no way resembled those of the record. In discharging him the Judge characterized the testimony as "the most startling proof of human fallibility" he had ever seen.

Fingerprint evidence is good evidence and should be carefully preserved by the police officer, man or woman.

MISSING PERSONS AND UNIDENTIFIED

CHAPTER XI

MISSING PERSONS AND THE UNIDENTIFIED

THE first policewoman New York City
ever had was originally assigned to
work in the Bureau of Missing Persons and
Unidentified Dead. This bureau had been
established soon after the disappearance of
Ruth Cruger, whose body was subsequently
found buried in a cellar in one of New York's
busy and populous sections. The appointment of a policewoman as well as the found-
ing of this bureau were practically out-
growths of this one time baffling mystery,
for in it was demonstrated the need of a better system for locating missing persons, as well
as the necessity of having women to handle
the cases of young girls and women.

It is an amazing fact that the number of

missing persons reported in the City of New York yearly approximates thirteen thousand, while on an average, six hundred unidentified bodies are recovered. Since nearly seventy-five per cent of the missing persons are between the ages of fifteen and twenty-two and two-thirds of them females, there is indeed a big field for policewomen—the task of finding missing girls not only in New York, but everywhere.

"Wilful—missing," a term used by Kipling in portraying the deserters from the British Army, aptly describes the average missing person. With a few rare exceptions the person who disappears and cannot be found does not want to be found.

A great deal has been said about the dangers of the City. To many people New York is a fierce monster ready to swallow the innocent girl or woman. Danger in any city does not exist for the woman or girl who does right and tends to her own business. A woman alone can go about New York at any hour of the twenty-four without being exposed to serious insult or real bodily peril, provided she shows by her conduct that she is not interested in anything except her own affairs.

A man of long experience in handling missing persons cases once declared that it is impossible to kidnap any girl from a New York street "if she has a mouth with which she can holler."

Of course a person may become ill or suffer an accident and being without identification remain temporarily "missing." But unless persons are ill or dead, they can be located by the police within a reasonable time provided they are not themselves frustrating the search.

Formerly little attention was given to the problem of the missing persons in New York City. These cases were simply reported to nine branches of the Detective Bureau which meant that the search for the person was necessarily undertaken by a detective, who, in all probability, was already overtaxed with work on many important criminal cases involving murder, burglary, larceny and lesser crimes.

Consequently he could not devote very much time to a search for a missing person and often had to file a case without having solved the mystery. As a last resort a general alarm was sent out, but as the alarm sheets contained hundreds of cases varying in degree, character and importance, no detective could give any particular case special attention.

It was customary then to report only the more serious missing person cases or important cases of unidentified dead, so under the old system hundreds of cases failed to receive any police attention whatsoever.

With the establishment of a central bureau for the location of missing persons and the identification of the dead it is possible to investigate thoroughly every case reported and to specialize in missing persons and the unidentified. The system now followed in New

York City can be adopted by any city or town. It is simple and efficient.

A missing person card is made out for every missing person and an unknown dead card for every unidentified dead person. When a person is reported missing a search is immediately made in the unidentified file. If any one answering the description is found the persons interested in the case are requested to go to the morgue to view the body and examine the effects of the deceased. Frequently they come to the bureau to see the photograph of the unidentified. If a file contains no description of the person reported, a card is made out on the case and filed for future reference.

In interviewing friends and relatives regarding missing persons, it is necessary to conduct the conferences in a private, confidential way. A request for no publicity should always be respected, but the fact that publicity is one of the most expedient means of finding the person should be pointed out and a big effort made to convince the parents or friends of the necessity of advertising their loss.

Description is relied upon mainly for the identification, and it is most important that an accurate and complete description is given, whether the person be living or dead. In a large number of cases it is difficult to secure detailed information. A mother, for instance, is frequently unable to tell the exact color of her daughter's hair; a father does not know the height or weight of his son. Recently a man who had been married ten years stated that he had no idea of the color of his wife's eyes. If descriptions are accurate, the search is made more easily and quickly.

It is also important that the name of the person reported missing be spelled correctly. A woman named Dirchen was reported as missing. A policeman found her wandering on the street, recorded her as Derchen. At the hospital she was registered as Durchen and when transferred to another hospital was listed as Doerchen. Had not the person investigating her case searched for her under every possible spelling of her name, she might not have been found speedily.

The cards containing information in reference to the missing are filed in folders according to age. The classification is as follows: From one to ten years, ten to fifteen, fifteen to twenty, twenty to thirty, etc. All cards are filed in the respective folders according to the date of disappearance. So accurate is the card system that over one-fourth of the dead are identified by means of these cards alone. Many unconscious persons in hospitals are also identified in this way. An unidentified woman was sent to a hospital and reported as follows: Thirty-two years old, brown hair, gray eyes, "brown velvet dress;" says "Jennie Smith." Search in the missing file failed to reveal any one named "Jennie Smith" or any one answering her description. The following day, however, one Sophie Reed was reported missing; description as follows: Thirty years old, brown hair, gray eyes and "brown velvet dress." When the folder containing the records of missing persons thirty years of age was consulted, it was found that "Jennie Smith" answered the description of Sophie Reed. Thereupon the mother of the woman was notified and she was able to identify her.

Three other means are used in tracing a person, the photograph, the laundry file and the never-failing finger-impression. The latter comes into play particularly when the unidentified or missing have a previous court record. With universal fingerprinting every person could be identified this way.

The following interesting case illustrates the use of the photograph: The body of an unidentified woman was recovered—she having been drowned in the river. Search in the missing persons' record failed to reveal any clue as to her identity. The detective who examined the body declared that the woman was without doubt a cook, and based his decision upon these facts: The victim was clad in a house dress; her sleeves were rolled up to the elbows, indicating that she had just left her work; the thumb, forefinger and middle finger of her left hand bore the marks of potato stains, the cuticle of these fingers had been cut with a paring knife, which she had doubtless held in her right hand, because there was a callous spot between the thumb and forefinger of her right hand. Moreover, her feet were calloused, indicating that she had stood on them a great deal.

As she was not the usual type of river victim, it was thought that she would be identified within a few days, yet her picture remained in the gallery for over a year, and still no inquiry was made regarding her. One day, by chance, an insurance man who was calling at the bureau mentioned the disappearance of a cook who had worked in a large downtown hospital, stating that nothing had been heard of her for over a year. He was amazed when told that the person of whom he spoke was doubtless the *cook* whose photograph was in the gallery. This incident made it possible to get in touch with relatives of the deceased, and inform them of her death. Many similar discoveries are made, often weeks or months after the death. The files of the missing and unidentified remain active until the case is satisfactorily closed by locating the missing, or securing the identification of the dead.

The value of the laundry file in the bureau's efforts to discover the identity of a person can scarcely be measured. Prior to the establishment of the bureau, a man who had been killed by a trolley car was buried in the city cemetery, because there appeared to be no means of identifying him. He had not been reported missing. Subsequently (and this very incident shows the need of the bureau's cooperating with other cities and towns, nationalizing its efforts, so to speak, and hence broadening the scope and effectiveness of its service), a woman in a southern city who had heard of the good work that the bureau was doing, wrote for information regarding her son. She said that he had been employed in a hotel in New York City, and as it was his custom to write to her every week, she was greatly alarmed about him, because she had not heard from him in several months. Inquiry was made at the hotel, where it was learned that the man had disappeared several months previously. His clothing, which had been placed in a bag in the hotel's store-room was examined. The bag contained several pieces that had been laundered. The laundry mark was Lx-311x. Search of the clothing of the unidentified at the morgue revealed a collar, belonging to the man who had been killed in the trolley accident, bearing the same indicator and number. His name was later verified at the laundry. Now every laundry indicator is filed at the Bureau of Missing Persons. As each laundry has its own indicator, and every customer is given a number, it is possible to effect an identification of many persons who might otherwise be buried as unknown.

Many bodies are identified in other unique ways; peculiar teeth, watches, clothing labels, buttons, pins, emblems, keys, eyeglasses, patches on their shoes or clothing. Recently a body that had been lying on the bottom of Kill von Kull for four months was recovered. The shoes of the victim were too large and had been stuffed with newspaper; by this clue alone the man was identified.

Search for a missing person sometimes extends all over the world. Recently, in the case of a sixteen-year-old girl, search was carried on between New York and Chicago; to San Francisco and Seattle; again to San Francisco, China, Japan, and back again to San Francisco, thence to Chicago once more; to New York, Boston, Troy and back once more to Chicago; there she was finally located in the suburbs of the city, where she was living —happily married.

The scope of the work and the volume of

correspondence resulting in the bureau's efforts to communicate with the proper authorities in other cities indicates the need for the establishment of a National Exchange Bureau of Missing Persons and Unidentified Dead, whereby the information obtained in one city may be readily communicated to similar agencies in other cities, who, in turn, would assist by forwarding such information as they might have regarding cases.

Every missing persons bureau should have at its disposal an emergency fund to cover extra expenses that arise from time to time. Often in working on these cases, the investigators are obliged to pay car fares, buy extra meals for their charges, and even provide clothing for the missing persons before returning them to their homes.

It is essential that the Bureau of Missing Persons be notified of the return of a prodigal. Parents, who so readily report a girl as missing, often forget to inform the police when she returns home of her own accord. This means that a staff of workers are wasting time and money in a futile search. While it is always advisable to report a case of disappearance so that action may be taken without delay, many cases are reported too hastily by over anxious parents. A girl may go to a dance and instead of returning home as she should, remains at a girl friend's house. The first thing in the morning the frantic mother reports her as missing, quite forgetting to close the case at Police Headquarters when the girl returns home later in the day.

Some cases receive wider newspaper publicity than others. Certainly no single case was more widely broadcast than that of Dorothy Arnold. Aside from the spectacular news story of the missing person, a few newspapers daily publish free of charge a missing persons column. This is exceedingly helpful to anyone engaged in the search.

The part that the policewoman plays in the tragic drama of the missing person strikes a deep human note. To the anguished mother who waits and waits for the return of her daughter, a woman's sympathy eases the sorrow and establishes a bond that the matter of fact man detective could never hope to approach.

And then again—the girl problem, when the policewoman finds the "wilful missing" daughter and has to persuade her to return home, not without a struggle, by appealing to her as woman to woman.

Statistics show that more women disappear than men. Because of her physiological make-up many small unaccountable things upset a woman to the extent of causing her to disappear suddenly without leaving any trace. Once she finds herself removed from her old environment, her mind clears, her small grievances or family disputes lose their immense importance and she is able to resume her old place. She returns home.

A very small proportion of missing persons are never found. To be sure some remain away for fifteen or twenty years but most of them disappear for only a few days. Every day, however, in every great city a certain number of people leave home and never come back. Nothing is heard from them again. The anxiety that they cause their family and friends is probably worse than if they had died.

Only by expanding this work of locating missing persons and seeking an identification of the unknown dead can the port of missing men, women, girls and boys be cleared of its thousand tragedies. Policewomen can help in this great and good work—truly a work for women.

WOMEN AND CHILDREN IN CRIME

CHAPTER XII

WOMEN AND CHILDREN IN CRIME

THE bestborn child in the world would doubtless become the worst criminal were he placed in a bad home to be reared by criminal parents. Most criminals are made, not born, and it is bad environment that makes them. Study the case histories of any group of prison inmates and it will be found that invariably behind the prison record is a long series of reformatory records, and preceding that a period of unsupervised street life and bad home conditions.

An enormous amount of public money is spent yearly in the apprehension, prosecution and punishment of criminals. If the same amount of money were expended in checking the tide of criminality the volume of crime would soon decrease.

In one case out of a hundred the penal and correctional institutions, as they exist today, may accomplish a reformation, but if there is ever going to be any substantial and lasting reduction of crime, it must begin with the children. They must never be allowed to become criminals.

A child who is handicapped before he is born is a potential criminal. Harmful hereditary influences are contributory factors in the creation of a criminal. If added to a weak constitution a child is compelled to live in an unwholesome environment with no strong guiding hand to help him over the rough places, his destiny is assured. Prison is just ahead.

A policewoman who corrects a vicious environment is saving boys and girls from lives of crime and this is exactly what a policewoman does do. There are other anti-social dangers, backwardness, truancy, incorrigibility and associability, which, if not detected during early childhood become definite causes of crime. To correct these before they become fixed is the duty of the public schools today. If our children are to be saved for the good of society every one must join together—the parents, the teachers and all community workers. To this group belongs the policewoman.

Within the past few years there has been a decided increase in crime and the new criminals are largely recruited from among women and children. Never before was the policewoman more greatly needed, for by her prevention policy alone can the child be rescued from a life of crime, while in the case of the woman, the kind of protection that the policewoman offers may swerve a girl from the downward path, particularly if she is a young, first offender.

There have always been women criminals, for crime is simply an expression of human weakness, from which men and women alike suffer. The appalling situation today is the fact that there are so many more women criminals and that the crimes committed by women are so desperate and scientifically planned. Crime has actually become a profession for women. To allow women to degenerate in this wholesale fashion is a more serious menace to society than if the new offenders were men, for the woman criminal may also be a mother and her influence on the offspring is usually closer and more vital than that of the father. In order to decrease crime among children it is sometimes necessary to begin before birth so that it will not be possible for a mother to endow her child with criminal tendencies. A baby born in prison marks a failure against civilization in the neglect of its duty to provide a clean, wholesome birthright for every child. An indication of the crime wave of women is revealed in the recent numerous and frequent occurrences of prison births.

In curbing crime among women, it is essential to determine the causes that are compelling them to become bandits, gangsters and desperados. It will be found that the driving forces in crime today are chiefly economic, while social and psychological elements also figure among the reasons why women choose crime for a career.

The modern woman wants money, for money signifies luxury and ease. Some women obtain this end through marriage, others take up serious professions and thereby win economic freedom. The woman criminal fights, kills and steals in order that she may possess all the good things that the modern world has to offer. She must have money and she gets it in whatever way she can.

The woman of today has more freedom than her grandmothers had and consequently there is a bigger opportunity for her to pursue any activity that she wishes to undertake whether it be a legitimate profession or a questionable career. The modern woman of sixteen or sixty is looking for a thrill, and to the primitive, untrained mind, crime carries with it the excitement that, in her restlessness, this sort of woman craves.

The modern drama, the moving picture and current fiction have popularized the woman crook to a certain extent, so that she does not appear so completely in the light of an outcast of society. In seeking a thrill the young, impressionable girl is very apt to mould her life according to the ways of the demimonde, if this is "the ideal" that has been presented to her through as influential a medium as the stage, screen or press.

Shifting social standards have taken away much of the restraint that was formerly placed upon women. A woman of poise and judgment knows how to use her new freedom, but the unwise and ruthless woman throws conventions to the four winds in her wild pursuit towards the selfish object of her goal. The crimes of women today are characterized by a decided lack of restraint and unmoral sense.

There are two constructive ways of lessening crime among women. The first cure rests in the proper education of girls and women. This means better home training, better economic training and a stronger spiritual and moral training. To accomplish this it is not advisable to go back to the repression of former generations, but rather to base all training upon self-expression, judgment and high ideals.

The policewoman can discover the pitfalls and scientifically treat the breeding places of crime; it remains for the other good servants of society to carry on the fight against crime with equally as firm and strong a purpose.

The second solution of crime, as it concerns women, is enforcement. The average judge and jury today is too easy with a woman. A woman commits murder; she is acquitted in nine cases out of ten, not on the facts but on the fact that she is a woman. Not until women learn what the real price of crime is, will they who have entered the profession decide that the carrying charges are too costly for them to risk.

[157]

PUBLICITY

CHAPTER XIII

PUBLICITY

IN police circles there are two schools of thought about the subject of publicity. One group believes that the best police work is done by throwing upon the careers of criminals the glaring light of publicity, while the others think that it is essential to plod along without the help of the press.

In some instances it is necessary to maintain secrecy until a case reaches a certain stage of development but in general the work of policewomen is such that the more publicity given it, the better it progresses.

Take as an illustration any kidnapping case. How far would the police get, if the newspapers did not blare forth the story of the grief stricken mother, the frenzied father and every detail regarding the lost child. As a result, clues and clues are offered, some valueless to be sure, others exposing conditions which require police attention, a few leading directly to the solution of the case. Without a doubt Lillian Rosen, who was kidnapped by a woman whose reputation is that of an international kidnapper, several years ago in New York City, owes her safe return home to the newspapers. Every clue, most of them being the fruits of newspaper publicity, was investigated. Finally a young girl reading the story of the crime reported that she believed she had seen the child with her abductor in a certain neighborhood. This clue led directly to the recovery of the child.

There is no surer means of locating a missing person than through the newspapers. Sometimes a person returns home voluntarily when he reads the account of his strange disappearance. Again another person will recognize the missing person and give a clue as to his whereabouts upon seeing a picture in the paper.

A condition that cannot bear the light of publicity should not exist. In preventing crime and protecting children, girls and women, the newspaper is a medium that can be used by the policewoman to point out the many evils that threaten their welfare. Moving pictures and the radio are also instruments through which appeals may be made to people. The great mass of public opinion largely determines the policewoman's policy and it is the newspaper that creates this vital force.

Sometimes personal publicity becomes a target at which the critics aim. From the point of view of the policewoman personal publicity is invaluable. It is well for her to get as much of it as she can, to be in the limelight as much as possible. Why? Not to satisfy vanity or selfish desires, but to become so well known that the timidest mother will write to her confidentially and ask for aid in finding the missing daughter; that all people with problems, knowing about her and having read what she has done for others, will seek her help. The policewoman must be well known.

The American Press is a big, brave, mighty, fair institution. If one is doing the right thing, he has no reason to fear it. It is a friend. The editors and the reporters, both men and women, have done a great deal to further the policewoman movement. They always accept a good thing.

Policewomen should cooperate with the press; give it your story and in return you will find that it will give you and your work good publicity, good service and great help.

PROTECTION AND CRIME
PREVENTION

CHAPTER XIV

PROTECTION AND CRIME PREVENTION

THE idea of protection is the very essence of a policewoman's duty. She is the guardian of life and property in the community just as the policeman is, only she protects in a more subtle unseen way.

If a policewoman is to be an effective protective officer for children, girls and women, she must know the world in which they live, the social and economic conditions of the neighborhood and the agencies with whom she will cooperate in the course of her work.

A district is determined by its boundaries, and characterized by its population, housing, industries, churches and schools. In many cities certain sections possess peculiar customs and traditions which distinguish them from all other vicinities and these differences produce social and economic problems which in no way resemble those of other communities even within a few city blocks. New York with its vast foreign population is a typical example of cosmopolitan community life and organization. As a result New York copes with situations that a great city like London, for instance, is never called upon to face. The foreign population of any American city presents difficult problems, problems of education, housing, labor, Americanization and finally the problems of protection and crime prevention.

The immigrant, for many reasons, may be the victim of the unscrupulous. His ignorance of the language and customs of the country render him easy prey for dwellers of the underworld, many of whom are his own countrymen. Then too, under the present immigration system, it is possible for persons with criminal tendencies and in some cases even those with criminal records to enter the United States, for as yet no truly selective policy has been adopted.

It is a significant fact that a large proportion of our young criminals today are born of foreign parentage. The first generation of foreigners, the immigrants themselves, are usually hard working and industrious. The second generation, their children, unless they are brought under right influences, seem to become intoxicated with American freedom, to the extent of disregarding their parents' ideals completely and substituting for them the code of the gang.

This vast body of future American citizens live for the most part in crowded tenements with the street as their playground. Early in life they come within reach of the law and it is the police officer, who being brought in daily contact with these children, can extend to them a protection that will preserve for them their old world heritage and keep untarnished the new world opportunity.

Police protection and crime prevention,

while reaching individuals in a personal way
through the safeguarding of homes and public
streets, concentrates upon the crowd or group.
Proper protection by policewomen for children, girls and women and the prevention of
crime among this group, necessitates the safeguarding of recreation centers, for just as
surely as all work and no play make Jack a
dull boy, so the wrong sort of play makes him
a very bad boy.

Danger lurks in parks, playgrounds,
beaches, piers, and baths unless there is some
one to watch over these pleasure haunts experienced enough to recognize a devastating
evil, however well disguised. It is the policewoman who possesses this observation and
insight.

Far greater are the hazards of commercial
recreation centers. Dance halls, skating
rinks, moving picture theatres, pool parlors,
ice cream saloons, cafés, cabarets, and amusement parks all may become crime centers, if
they are not, by careful inspection and super-

vision, kept fit for the young people who patronize them. This is a task for which the policewoman is qualified, for she has the power to enforce law and unobserved may mingle with the pleasure seekers without arousing suspicion. So closely may she approach the danger points that often she literally saves a girl just as she is about to take the fatal step.

In protecting society against crime especially in preserving the safety of girls and women, the automobile figures conspicuously as an agency of crime to be combatted. The automobile is indispensable to the criminal both as a lure and as a means whereby he may make a quick getaway.

A man with a car makes a strong appeal to the pleasure craving, romantic young girl who, alas, usually believes too firmly in a short life and a merry one. Many men today use a car as an inducement in "picking up" girls. They "cruise" along the prominent thoroughfares of large cities seeking to entice foolish girls who see no harm in a little flirtation. To the man any woman who accepts his advances is a potential prostitute; the average girl thinks of nothing beyond the fun of a joy-ride.

That the story of the girl found unconscious by the road recurs from time to time indicates that the automobile danger still exists and shows the need of greater effort on the part of parents, teachers and protective officers to eliminate this menace.

Another phase of the automobile evil is the taxicab. It is essential that a public utility such as this be freed from the perils that threaten it when it is possible for men with criminal records, ex-convicts many of them, to secure licenses permitting them to follow the taxi driving trade. To bring these applicants directly within the supervision of the police would assure to the public the protection that it needs to fight one phase of the taxicab danger.

A prominent organization interested in the

suppression of vice, made the appalling statement in its annual report several years ago that the taxicab is "running the hotels a close second as a place where immorality is carried on." The responsibility for such conditions rests to some extent with the taxicab companies, who should engage drivers capable of checking irregularities of any sort. It is also a matter of public concern and should be treated by the police as an offense against public decency.

As a protective and crime preventive measure it is of vital importance to have some conveniently located agency equipped to furnish information to the stranger, the citizen in distress and the person ignorant of danger. The police fulfill this need to some extent, but their activity in this direction is necessarily more or less cursory. They are, however, the logical agency to assume this duty and since the men are already overburdened with work, it seems feasible for the women of the police to develop this activity as a distinct phase of

[173]

policewomen's work. During the war a group of women rendered excellent service along this line in conducting the information booths established by the War Camp Community Service. To have policewomen, protective officers, permanently stationed at prominent points throughout any big community including the railroad* and steamship terminals would be the means of saving many unfortunate people who through ignorance, weakness or distraction are lead into trouble which may later develop into crime. Women doing this kind of police duty should, contrary to the general rule, wear uniforms to distinguish and identify them as persons of official authority.

In developing a program of crime prevention and protection, policewomen can find no better institution through which to work than the public school. It has been indicated that the hope of the ultimate prevention of crime

---

*The Charter of the City of New York includes this service among police duties and functions.

depends upon the proper education of the younger generation. Today the subject of fire prevention is taught in our schools. Protection and crime prevention equally concern human life and happiness and should have a place in the curriculum of daily affairs.

If every school had a woman protective officer, a policewoman, to handle its difficult girls and boys and teach all children the fundamentals of crime prevention, there would be fewer juvenile delinquents and less crime. Every other officer dealing with children acts when the harm has been done. The policewoman has the advantage of being able to deal with the child before he becomes an offender against society.

THE POLICEWOMAN AND
THE LAW

CHAPTER XV

THE POLICEWOMAN AND THE LAW

IT is a sad sight on a beautiful spring day to see a little boy being led off to a police-station lugging a baseball bat and other sporting paraphernalia. In playing ball on the streets he violates a law, to be sure, but arrest is a poor solution for his particular offense against society. Although policewomen as officers of the law are empowered with the authority to make arrests whenever the law has been disregarded, they exercise this right with caution and resort to this means of enforcement as a last resort.

Such an attitude on their part does not signify laxity, but rather expresses the policy that women police have adopted in seeking to make their program of protection and crime prevention an actual force in the community. Any policewoman who is true to these ideals would not drag a child into court because he played ball. She would warn him against breaking the law, watch him closely to see that he did not do so again and ultimately solve the whole problem by providing a proper playground for him.

It would be a simple matter for the policewoman to terminate the case of a difficult girl whose acts barely escape delinquency by making an arrest and bringing her within the jurisdiction of the court. By careful, tactful handling, such cases can be settled between the policewoman and the girl without the intervention of the court. Just as the probation officer watches over the welfare of children once they have made a false step, so the policewoman can watch over those who are about to take the leap.

A young girl whom a policewoman had befriended was eager to have a friend brought under her good influence. "I know you can

help her," she said, "but please don't tell her
you're a policewoman, not until she finds out
how good you are. It might scare her before
she knows that you really are a friend." This
homely bit of feminine wisdom might well
apply to the policewomen and her power to
arrest. It is better not to frighten away those
whom she would help and protect by reveal-
ing a weapon that could be used against the
offenders. A policewoman of long experience
is proud of the fact that she has still to make
her first arrest. Of course there have been oc-
casions in the course of her service when arrests have been necessary, but is has been her
policy to have this part of the job done by the
man, in order that her reputation as a friend
and protector may be maintained.

For a policewoman to know and understand the laws that she is called upon to enforce is absolutely necessary. Ignorance of
law excuses no one, but for a policewoman
not to know what the law is would be gross,
inexcusable ignorance.

In mastering so intricate a subject, the beginner can · start by learning the rules and regulations of the department of which she is a part. Then, as in any other modern, progressive profession, further knowledge can be gained only by hard and continuous study. The law itself is one of the important tools of a policewoman's trade.

In the course of a policewoman's duties she is brought in contact with the courts usually in the capacity of a witness. The quality of her testimony has weight in so far as it is accurate, straightforward and unprejudiced. The impression that women officers make at those times is far reaching. Their conduct in the court room should be dignified and womanly, for from it public opinion regarding them is molded.

Policewomen and probation officers each function in a different sphere, the one before, the other after the crime. Sometimes a policewoman's interest in a case will extend beyond the point where her authority ends. If such is the case there is no reason why she and the probation officer should not join forces and work the problem out together, for a child on probation is returned to society where again he comes within the protective jurisdiction of the policewoman.

A good policewoman never hounds a probationer, but in keeping her eye on him she can often save him from a second misstep or keep him within the bounds of his probation.

The policewoman has been likened to the mother. Hers is the strong arm of the law as it is expressed in a woman's guiding hand.

COOPERATION AMONG
POLICEWOMEN

CHAPTER XVI

COOPERATION AMONG POLICEWOMEN

POLICE work, as it is done by women, is a social service requiring the cooperation of all policewomen, social agencies and people whose interests center in the welfare of human beings.

Policewomen, the world over, are working toward the same end, the betterment of human condition through protection and crime prevention and to accomplish what they have set out to do, they must join forces and fight crime as a unit not in weak, individual combat.

To attain group strength, the organization of the women police must begin to knit firmly at its base, the policewoman force of each town or city. From such a union can be

[187]

developed the federation of women police in all cities, culminating in a big cooperative congress in which policewomen from every part of the world will be represented.

While much of a policewoman's service is purely local, there are times when the cases that she handles carry her beyond immediate domain of her particular precinct. She is called upon to deal with a runaway girl from a distant city and the success or failure of her task is determined largely by the degree of cooperation and understanding that she is able to secure from her colleagues in the home town of her charge. Again in the solution of a missing person case, she may seek the aid of every policewoman in the world.

Aside from the professional cooperation, the policewoman is daily brought in contact with social agencies of all kinds with whom she must establish friendly relation in order fully to produce the results that are possible with the modern machinery that present day organizations have set up to solve social problems. So familiar should a policewoman be with the social service agencies of her community that it would be impossible for any matter to arise that she could not immediately refer to the proper authority.

Few policemen have a practical training in social service. A typical case was demonstrated recently where a destitute mother and child appealed to a policeman in a large city for food and shelter at night. Out of the kindness of his heart he took them to numerous institutions, none of whom, for technical reasons could admit them. He did not know what any social worker could have told him, that a joint application bureau, open day and night, existed in that city to meet such an emergency.

Effective police work demands public support. There have been times when the police have failed to win the approbation of the people and have been subjected to severe criticism with the effect of diminishing their moral force and depleting personal efficiency.

The cause of the policewoman is a popular one, which claims the attention of the public and invariably wins its approval. The woman, symboling the mother, stands for the protection of home and family—an ideal for which mankind throughout the history of the world have given their lives. The success of women police work is a story of public cooperation.

Police departments which find themselves at odds with the public should put forth the woman's cause, if they wish to win back the faith of the people, for the people have shown that they have faith in policewomen.

PITFALLS

CHAPTER XVII

PITFALLS

THE policewoman is a pilgrim whose path is beset by many obstacles and pitfalls. Unless she has a firm purpose, a clear idea of her program, an understanding of the methods that she must use to accomplish her aims and high ideals to lift her above petty attempts to discredit her value, she will fail to render the effective service that she, as a woman, is capable of contributing to a cause which needs her viewpoint, intuition and unfailing spirit.

Politics are a pitfall that the policewoman must avoid early in her career. Party leaders cannot dictate to one whose policy embraces all and all alike. Protection and Crime Prevention are ideals beyond petty politics. A policewoman must be free to pursue

[193]

her tasks unhampered by the limitation that politics place upon one.

Playing politics to secure an appointment immediately obligates the policewoman to render unto politics the things that are politics and such things are not always her ideals.

Another pitfall is the System. It can quickly submerge the person who enters it with the idea of treating the work as a job to be done with the least possible effort and the greatest possible ease. Getting on the right side of somebody; doing underhanded work, are all mill stones around the neck of a woman. To such a person policewomanship does not reach beyond the realm of the routine.

A woman entering any police department for the first time, must necessarily comply with the rules and regulations; they are sensible and fair. She does not, however, have to adhere to any customs that revolt against her ideals. The old time policeman uses the phrase "covering himself." In it is expressed all the fear of being brought up on charges.

Pitfalls

The minute the policewoman begins "to cover herself" she is enveloping her ideals in the meshes of the System. A woman must blaze her own trail and while considering her colleagues of the old school, work independently of them when it comes to the point of doing the work of a woman in the police field as a woman would do it.

The most dangerous pitfall is the one which narrows the mind into a single tract and limits the mental processes of the worker so that she cannot see things in true proportion. This is the industrial disease of police work, the result of suspicion and fear. A policewoman must maintain a mental poise if she expects to be a force for good. Right thinking helps both the thinker and the person whom the thinker would help. A good thought is magnetic; it reaches out, attracts and subjects the opposite force—evil.

There are no pitfalls that the policewoman cannot escape if she remains true to her service and ideals.

[195]

THE POLICEWOMAN OF THE FUTURE

CHAPTER XVIII

THE POLICEWOMAN OF THE FUTURE

THE policewoman of today in her service and ideals foreshadows the policewoman of the future. Courageously these pioneers have dedicated a monumental work for the benefit of mankind and laboriously laid the foundation for a permanent structure that will rise to the heights of achievement.

In the future there will be more policewomen. The field of service, however, will not change. Women protective officers will always confine their efforts to work with children, girls and women. Their slogan, Protection and Crime Prevention, will continue to motivate their activities and inspire them to accomplish greater good.

A few years will see the fulfillment of the

ideals that policewomen today hold and cherish. From a small, isolated group, women protective officers will rise to take their rightful places beside the men, cooperating with them, so that society may have the full benefit of a woman's point of view in solving those difficult problems that threaten the life and safety of mothers and children, the vital threads of the social fabric.

Crime is a super-social disease. The policewoman of today is doing the research work that will reveal its sources, causes and possible remedies. In the policewoman of the future rests the hope of a permanent and lasting cure.

POLICE IN AMERICA
An Arno Press/New York Times Collection

The American Institute of Law and Criminology.
Journal of the American Institute of Law and Criminology:
Selected Articles. Chicago, 1910–1929.

The Boston Police Strike: Two Reports. Boston, 1919–1920.

Boston Police Debates: Selected Arguments. Boston,
1863–1869.

Chamber of Commerce of the State of New York.
**Papers and Proceedings of Committee on the Police Problem,
City of New York.** New York, 1905.

Chicago Police Investigations: Three Reports. Illinois,
1898–1912.

Control of the Baltimore Police: Collected Reports.
Baltimore, 1860–1866.

Crime and Law Enforcement in the District of Columbia:
Report and Hearings. Washington, D. C., 1952.

Crime in the District of Columbia: Reports and Hearings.
Washington, D. C., 1935.

Flinn, John J. and John E. Wilkie.
History of the Chicago Police. Chicago, 1887.

Hamilton, Mary E.
The Policewoman. New York, 1924.

Harrison, Leonard Vance.
Police Administration in Boston. Cambridge, Mass., 1934.

International Association of Chiefs of Police.
Police Unions. Washington, D. C., 1944.

The Joint Special Committee.
**Reports of the Special Committee Appointed to Investigate
the Official Conduct of the Members of the Board of Police
Commissioners.** Boston, 1882.

Justice in Jackson, Mississippi: U.S. Civil Rights
Commission Hearings. Washington, D. C., 1965.

McAdoo, William.
Guarding a Great City. New York, 1906.

Mayo, Katherine.
Justice to All. New York, 1917.

Missouri Joint Committee of the General Assembly.
**Report of the Joint Committee of the General Assembly
Appointed to Investigate the Police Department of the
City of St. Louis.** St. Louis, Missouri, 1868.

National Commission on Law Observance and Enforcement.
Report on the Police. Washington, D. C., 1931.

National Prison Association.
**Proceedings of the Annual Congress of the National Prison
Association of the United States: Selected Articles.**
1874–1902.

New York City Common Council.
**Report of the Special Committee of the New York City
Board of Aldermen on the New York City Police Department.**
New York, 1844.

National Police Convention.
Official Proceedings of the National Prison Convention.
St. Louis, 1871.

Pennsylvania Federation of Labor.
The American Cossack. Washington, D. C., 1915.

Police and the Blacks: U.S. Civil Rights Commission
Hearings. 1960–1966.

Police in New York City: An Investigation. New York,
1912–1931.

The President's Commission on Law Enforcement and
Administration of Justice.
Task Force Report: The Police. Washington, D. C., 1967.

Sellin, Thorsten, editor.
The Police and the Crime Problem. Philadelphia, 1929.

Smith, Bruce, editor.
New Goals in Police Management. Philadelphia, 1954.

Sprogle, Howard O.
The Philadelphia Police, Past and Present. Philadelphia,
1887.

U.S. Committee on Education and Labor.
The Chicago Memorial Day Incident: Hearings and Report.
Washington, D. C., 1937.

U.S. Committee on Education and Labor.
**Documents Relating to Intelligence Bureau or Red Squad of
Los Angeles Police Department.** Washington, D. C., 1940.

U.S. Committee on Education and Labor.
Private Police Systems. Washington, D. C., 1939.

Urban Police: Selected Surveys. 1926–1946.

Women's Suffrage and the Police: Three Senate Documents.
Washington, D. C., 1913.

Woods, Arthur.
Crime Prevention. Princeton, New Jersey, 1918.

Woods, Arthur.
Policeman and Public. New Haven, Conn., 1919.

AMERICAN POLICE SUPPLEMENT

International Association of Chiefs of Police.
Proceedings of the Annual Conventions of the International Association of Chiefs of Police. 1893–1930. 5 vols.

New York State Senate.
Report and Proceedings of the Senate Committee Appointed to Investigate the Police Department of the City of New York. (Lexow Committee Report). New York, 1895. 6 vols.

THE POLICE IN GREAT BRITAIN

Committee on Police Conditions of Service.
Report of the Committee on Police Conditions of Service. London, 1949.

Committee on the Police Service.
Minutes of Evidence and Report: England, Wales, Scotland. London, 1919–1920.

Royal Commission on Police Powers and Procedures.
Report of the Royal Commission on Police Powers and Procedure. London, 1929.

Select Committee on Police.
Report of Select Committee on Police with the Minutes of Evidence. London, 1853.

Royal Commission Upon the Duties of the Metropolitan Police.
Minutes of Evidence Taken Before the Royal Commission Upon the Duties of the Metropolitan Police Together With Appendices and Index. London, 1908.

Committee on Police.
Report from the Select Committee on Police of the Metropolis. London, 1828.